Archibald H. Sayce, Ernst von Bunsen

The Chronology of the Bible

connected with contemporaneous events in the history of Babylonians, Assyrians

and Egyptians

Archibald H. Sayce, Ernst von Bunsen

The Chronology of the Bible
connected with contemporaneous events in the history of Babylonians, Assyrians and Egyptians

ISBN/EAN: 9783337248017

Printed in Europe, USA, Canada, Australia, Japan

Cover: Foto ©Lupo / pixelio.de

More available books at **www.hansebooks.com**

THE
CHRONOLOGY OF THE BIBLE.

LONDON: PRINTED BY
SPOTTISWOODE AND CO., NEW-STREET SQUARE
AND PARLIAMENT STREET

THE CHRONOLOGY OF THE BIBLE,

CONNECTED WITH

CONTEMPORANEOUS EVENTS

IN THE HISTORY OF

BABYLONIANS, ASSYRIANS, AND EGYPTIANS.

BY ERNEST DE BUNSEN.

WITH A PREFACE

BY

A. H. SAYCE, M.A.

FELLOW AND TUTOR OF QUEEN'S COLLEGE, OXFORD.

LONDON:
LONGMANS, GREEN, AND CO.
1874.

All rights reserved.

PREFACE.

AMONG the many services rendered by the decipherment of the ancient monuments of Egypt and Assyria, none perhaps is more important than the certain basis it has afforded for the restoration of the chronology of the past. A true chronology is the necessary skeleton and framework of history, the events of which cannot be rightly understood and made instructive until we know their exact order and succession. The Old Testament was for a long time the sole source from which a chronological system of early history could be extracted; and we now know how imperfect that source was. The last few years, however, have opened up unexpected stores of information. Much light has come from Egypt, and still more from Assyria. The civilisations of the Tigris and Euphrates were in closer connection with the traditions and annals of the Hebrews than was that of the Nile; and while the lists of eponymes enable us to fix the dates of the most important part of Assyrian history with absolute precision, the key-periods of Jewish and Israelitish history are just those which have been determined and settled by the evidence of the cuneiform inscriptions.

It is this fact which has made me presumptuous enough, at the request of the Author, to trespass upon the domains of professed chronologists, and to draw attention as well as I can to the new and striking views set forth in the present volume. The Assyrian student is sometimes obliged to handle matters of chronology; and it thus happened that I found myself forced to investigate the difficult chronological questions connected with the campaign of Sennacherib against Hezekiah. The result of a comparison of the native monuments with the phænomena presented by the Hebrew text seemed to me to leave no room for doubt that whereas the campaign of Sennacherib took place in B.C. 701, there was an earlier conquest of Judæa by Sargon ten years before (B.C. 711), in the fourteenth year of Hezekiah. My satisfaction was great at finding that M. de Bunsen had arrived at the same conclusion on wholly independent grounds and in accordance with his general scheme of chronology.

This scheme, it will be seen, is a complete whole, the several parts of which hang together like the stones of an arch. A correct interpretation of the facts of Jewish, Egyptian, and Babylonian history is shown to result in a perfect harmony and a series of remarkable synchronisms. The author begins with an original theory of his, subsequently confirmed by Professor Müller, of Basel, that Shemites were a compound of Japhethites and Hamites, or Aryans and non-Aryans; and submits a new confirmation of it in the thesis that what in Genesis is called the birth of Shem refers to, or at all events is directly connected with, the capture of Babylon by the Medes of Berosus, in 2458 B.C. Other reasons are assigned for regarding this year as the starting-point of Hebrew chronology and explaining ethnically the birth of Shem. This suggests another probable or possible synchronism, the correspondence of the exodus from Haran with the establishment of a fresh (Elamite) dynasty in Babylonia, whose first king may have been the Chedorlaomer of Genesis.

Now, the unhistorical character of the 1656 years between the Creation and the Deluge seems placed beyond all dispute; and if the period of 592 years from the Exodus to the building of the Temple can really be proved, St. Paul and Josephus must have derived their information upon this point from some unpublished source. Here, then, we are referred to the hidden wisdom, the verbal tradition of the initiated, which has already formed the subject of a special investigation by M. de Bunsen, and is the real centre of his present researches. These researches, however, find what may be called their concrete expression in a scheme of Hebrew chronology which can be verified by a comparison with the annals of Assyria and Babylonia. In this way the author works back to the chronology of Egypt, and, by fixing the year 928 B.C. as the fifth of Rehoboam and 948 B.C. as that of Shishak's accession, is able to date the Manethonian Dynasties both backwards and forwards. A series of noteworthy synchronisms is the result, among which may be mentioned the threefold synchronism for the Pharaoh of the Exodus and the sevenfold synchronism for the year 711. No liberties, it may be said, have been taken in bringing about this harmony; the author claims to have made the Biblical and Assyrian records tell their own tale, though the system of co-regencies may not altogether exclude criticism. Since, however, Shalmaneser mentions the name of Ahab among the confederacy defeated by him in 854 B.C., it would appear that the battles of Karkar and Ramoth-Gilead were fought in the same year, and that the fourth year of Ahab corresponded with the first of Jehoshaphat's sole regency, not of his reign.

Other points suggested in the course of the work will excite much interest and discussion. Entirely new theories are put forward in regard to the age of Ezra and the Feast of Purim, and to the possible presence of St. Peter in Rome in the ninth year after the Crucifixion. But the conclusions most calculated to provoke attention and controversy are those connected with the life of Christ. Reasons are given for accepting the statement of Irenæus and regarding Jesus as in his forty-ninth year when he died. His birth is placed fourteen years before the Christian Era, and the wisdom which astonished the doctors at Jerusalem in a boy of twelve years of age is traced back to the schools of Alexandria.

I feel fully how very inadequate the preceding sketch of the contents of the present volume must be. But I have already stated my excuse for having undertaken to describe them; and I can only add my wish that they could have found a better hierophant. Much of the book trenches upon the province of the Assyriologue; and here at least I may be permitted to speak. The rest must be left to the judgment of others.

A. H. SAYCE.

Queen's College, Oxford.

INTRODUCTION.

THE science of language, and the discovered proofs of early civilisation, have established the fact that the Biblical Chronology, in the form transmitted to us, is too short, in its early periods, to allow us to regard it as strictly historical. Hence we must either assume that those who recorded the Chronology of Hebrew tradition were not sufficiently instructed in this branch of human knowledge, or that, for some reason or other, a designed alteration of traditional Chronology took place.

Hitherto, designed alterations have been proved in but two out of three records of the ancestors of Abraham, as contained in the Hebrew, the Greek, and the Samaritan texts. The spuriously inserted generation of the second 'Cainan' in the Septuagint is likewise found in the Gospel according to St. Luke. It has remained doubtful whether or not the genealogies in the Hebrew text have been preserved in accordance with historical tradition.[1]

Several and more important alterations of this kind can be detected in the Hebrew text with mathematical precision. As might be expected, we find them, not in any statement of detail, but in the record of two periods —of the period from Adam to the Flood, and in that

[1] See Mr. R. Stuart Poole's article on 'Chronology' in Dr. Smith's Dictionary of the Bible; also 'The Genesis of the Earth and Man,' p. 92.

from the Exodus to the building of the Temple. It will be shown that the Biblical text transmitted to us, as regards these two periods, cannot have been fixed before the return from Babylon, and that Hebrew Chronology was shortened for dogmatic reasons.

If these assertions can be sufficiently substantiated, no revision of the Biblical text would be complete which did not eradicate such undoubtedly unhistorical alterations. This would be a step in the right direction. Though it will ever be impossible to decide whether and to what extent alterations of the original Biblical records were effected, and still less how they are to be interpreted, yet the removal of palpable errors, without making the Bible an infallible book, would render more universal the conviction that a 'good deposit' of Divinely revealed truths is therein contained—that the Word of God is in the Bible.

Only in one of the two instances just mentioned can the incorrect period be safely replaced by the correct period. We hope to prove that 592 years, instead of 480 years, must be reckoned from the Exodus to the building of the Temple; and that the Apostle Paul and Josephus drew from one and the same oral or non-written tradition when they corrected the recorded period of 480 years—the one directly, the other indirectly. The incorrect and abbreviated period of 1,656 years, from Adam to the Flood, may possibly be replaced by one of 8,225 years; but this is a mere hypothesis at present.

The historical part of Hebrew Chronology begins with the year 2458 B.C., and from this date the Chronological information of the Bible is absolutely continuous. The enlargement of the period from the Exodus to the building of the Temple by 112 years, permits us to regard as historical the entire Chronology referring to the time of the Judges, and to show that the judgeship of Samuel lasted thirty-two years. Shishak's accession occurred during the reign of Solomon, as the Bible requires it; and the first expedition of the Assyrians to Judæa, in the time of Sargon, but possibly under the leadership of his son and successor Sennacherib, perhaps his co-regent, can be proved to have taken place, in absolute harmony with the Biblical statement, in the fourteenth year of Hezekiah, that is, in the year 711 B.C., the year given to the expedition to Ashdod and Judah by the Assyrian annals, known to us from cuneiform inscriptions lately deciphered. But the recorded destruction of Sennacherib's army refers to the second Assyrian campaign to the land of Judah in 701 B.C. Sargon seems to have at least surrounded Jerusalem in 711, and the fusion of both accounts in the Hebrew records must be attributed to a design.

All synchronisms required by the Bible and Assyrian inscriptions can be proved. In connection with the year 711 B.C., we hope to establish a sixfold, if not a sevenfold synchronism, which may be regarded as the most remarkable historical coincidence of ancient history. If we succeed in proving, that after the necessary correction of two of its periods, Hebrew Chronology refers to consecutive events, and that it commences at least 4,331 years before the present time, the historical value of the earliest Biblical records will have been vindicated.

It has not pleased God to watch over the composition and preservation of the Bible in such a manner as to prevent the record of error and even the intentional perversion of truth. But His Holy Spirit will lead mankind into all Truth.

Corrections and Additions.

PAGE			
2	line 9,	*read*	Salah 2323–1890.
2	„ 17	„	Isaac 1908–1788.
3	„ 28f	„	that the period assigned to the patriarchs has been shortened to the sum total of years which each patriarch is recorded to have lived before the birth of his one recorded son.
4	„ 4	„	was not left to be followed.
4	„ 7	„	Seth was made to live ....
17	„ 36	„	is a work ....; add: see there for the connection of the Armenian Ararat with the East.
19	„ 23	„	Shiddim which was fought in 1979, 255 years after 2234.
20	„ 4	„	kings who ....
25	„ 9	„	the lepers lived ....
27	„ 33	„	The First Book of Kings.
27	„ 37	„	Note 2: 1 Kings vi. 1.
37	„ 1	„	We assert that a king was called by a name similar to Pul or Val, but that he was not the grandson of Shalmaneser of the Black Obelisk, the Val-lush of Assyrian Monuments, whom Professor Rawlinson has identified with Phalos, the name given to Pul in the Septuagint. This king certainly preceded Tiglat Pilesar, but he need not have been his immediate predecessor, which, according to our chronology, he cannot have been. If the Pul of the Bible came ....
44	„ 14	„	all synchronisms ....
49	„ 13	„	to the lists derived from Ctesias.
55	„ 20	„	the prophet Ahijah recognised in Jeroboam the future ruler of the ten tribes.
58	„ 7	„	Add note: 1 Sam. xxx. 11 need not here be considered.
58	„ 34	„	to Ahmes.
62	„ 38	„	days.
67	„ 5	„	taxing (literally 'registration,' which cannot be separated from a supposed subsequent census) was ....
67	„ 9	„	B.C. 4.
68	„ 28	„	B.C. 3.
72	„ 31	„	31 B.C.
77	„ 23	„	after Luke.
78	„ 4	„	33 A.D.
79	„ 17	„	41 or previously.
79	„		Note add: The passages Acts v. 12–42 and vi. 7 may be referred to the same time as iv. 4 and ii. 47.
82	„ 21	„	add: Other Christians, according to the Acts, visited Antioch before St. Peter and St. Paul; but Antioch is called 'the chair of Peter by the Syrian Baradæus, see Bodl. Libr. Cod. 140, 5.
93	„ 2–10		lower by one line the first five years of Jeroboam.
99	„ 15	„	Jeroboam.
110	„ 32	„	Jeremiah.
111	„ 2	„	Add: In Jer. xv. 1 the term 'to stand before' is used as to Moses and Samuel, the application to Samuel would require an explanation if it were at all certain that he was not a priest and possibly a high priest. Jeremiah does not use it as to himself (xv. 19) where the correct text is: 'if thou turnest, I will again let you be my servant.' Thus also it is not used as to Elijah (1 Kings xvii. 1), where read: 'the God of Israel whom I serve.'

CONTENTS.

	PAGE
Preface	v
Introduction	ix
The Problem	1
The Patriarchs and the Millennium	2
Possible Antediluvian Tradition of 8225 Years	8
The Birth of Shem	11
The Exodus from Haran	11
The Battle of Shiddim	12
The Pharaoh of Joseph	13
From the Death of Joseph to the Exodus	14
The Pharaoh of the Bondage	15
Ethnic Relations of the Hebrews	16
The Exodus from Egypt	25
Retrospect of Chronological Results	30
The Assyrian Annals	32
Assyrian and Hebrew Synchronisms	33
Restoration of Babylonian Dynasties	45
Origin of Babylonian and of Assyrian Power	46
Egyptian Chronology	49
Table of Egyptian Dynasties	60
Ezra and the Purim	61
Year of the Birth and Year of the Death of Jesus	66
Year of the Martyrdom of St. Stephen and St. James	79
St. Peter and Philo in Rome	80
Retrospect and Conclusion	83

APPENDIX.

	PAGE
Note I. The Unabbreviated Periods of Genesis from Adam to the Flood	92
Note II. Table of Hebrew Chronology from the Death of Solomon to the Destruction of the Temple	93
,, III. Biblical Authorities for the Length of Reigns in Judah and Israel	97
,, IV. Date of the Accession of Thothmes the Great	100
,, V. Shishak I. and Pausennes II. Co-Regents	106
,, VI. On Deiokes and Daiuccu	109
,, VII. Murder of Joshua and Zechariah	110

INDEX 119–138

CHRONOLOGICAL TABLES.

THE
CHRONOLOGY OF THE BIBLE

&c.

THE PROBLEM.

HAD THE HEBREWS an historical chronology before the time of Solomon? This is absolutely denied by some of the ablest chronologists, it is doubted by many, and it has not yet been proved by anyone. If these remarkable people were brought in contact alternately with the most civilised nations of ancient times, with the Egyptians, the Babylonians, and the Assyrians, and if these nations had historical chronologies, it is probable, at the outset, that the Israelites must have possessed an historical tradition.

This assumption will be raised to the dignity of a fact as soon as it shall have been proved that two of the chronological periods in Genesis are incorrect—that is, the most ancient period of 1656 years and that of 480 years. To prove this is our first object. We shall determine with mathematical precision that the scheme of 7000 years has led to the shortening of the time from Adam to the Flood to 1656 years, and implies the duration of 592 years, not of 480 years, for the period from the exodus to the foundation of the temple. If we succeed in proving this, the designed alteration of the periods of 1656 and of 480 years will be established beyond all reasonable doubt, and it will be shown that this alteration of Hebrew tradition cannot possibly have taken place before the time of Ezra.

THE PATRIARCHS AND THE MILLENNIUM.

We assume the date for the Noachian deluge to be 2360 B.C., a date the correctness of which will be proved.

Patriarchs before the Flood.		*Patriarchs after the Flood.*	
	B.C.		B.C.
Adam	4016–3086	Arphaxad	2358–1920
Seth	3886–2974	Salah	2223–1800
Enos	3781–2876	Eber	2203–1829
Cainan	3691–2781	Peleg	2259–2020
Mahalaleel	3621–2726	Reu	2229–1990
Jared	3556–2594	Serug	2197–1967
Enoch	3394–3029	Nahor	2167–2019
Methuselah	3329–2360	Terah	2138–1933
Lamech	3142–2365	Abraham	2008–1833
Noah	2960–2010	Isaac	1908–1786
Shem	2458–1858	Jacob	1909–1703
		Joseph	1816–1706
The Flood	2360	Moses	1643–1523

Whilst, according to the Hebrew text, Methuselah died a few months or days before the commencement of the Flood, this supposition is untenable according to the Greek text. In the Septuagint, to which Jesus and the Apostles generally referred, Methuselah is stated to have been alive fourteen years after the Flood. On the supposition that the Flood was universal, and all men perished except those saved in the Ark, we should have to assume an unrecorded miraculous intervention in favour of Methuselah.

Assuming the statements in Genesis about the duration of the lives of the patriarchs to be historical in the form given above, the period from Adam to Moses would be bridged over by the lives of exactly seven persons. For Methuselah lived 243 years with Adam, and he must have been able to relate to Noah and his sons the history about Eden, Adam and Eve, and the serpent, exactly as he had heard it from the lips of Adam. Thus instructed by the contemporary of Adam, Shem was able to transmit this tradition to Jacob during the fifty years that these chosen men lived together. Jacob could thus have been informed by a contemporary of Methuselah how this patriarch was either removed by a timely death in the year of the Flood, or how by an unrecorded miraculous intervention of Providence, and without joining the favoured party in the Ark, the man of 969 years escaped from the condign punishment of the Flood, his only son Lamech having died five years before him, at the age of 777 years. This 'holy' tradition, transmitted directly by Adam, Methuselah, and Shem, Jacob could transmit to his son Levi, whose daughter Jochebed could instruct in this patriarchal tradition her son Moses, the future lawgiver, who, according to Rabbinical tradition, was the founder of the institution of seventy elders, and whom he instructed in the oral tradition. This was the most important initiation of the man who was brought up in all the wisdom of the Egyptians. Hebrew tradition began to be written down in the time of Moses, but, by an uninterrupted succession, this 'holy' tradition went up to Adam. Like the house of divine wisdom, the house of holy tradition was built on seven pillars.[1]

We shall now show that the sum total of the duration of lives assigned to the patriarchs has been shortened by the sum total of the years which each patriarch is recorded to have lived together with his one recorded son. This latter sum total will be found to corre-

---

[1] Prov. ix. 1; comp. Gal. ii. 9. St. Peter was regarded as one of the 'pillars,' at the same time as 'the rock.' The wisdom of God (or the power of God) is implied to have 'hewn her pillars' from a rock. Christ, 'the power of God and the wisdom of God,' is called 'the spiritual rock which followed the Israelites.' 'The rock' is a symbolical expression for the Holy Ghost.

spond to the 1656 years which remained for the period from the Flood to Adam, if the scheme of 7000 years was to be supported by Hebrew chronology. The first period of 930 years called after Adam was not followed by the period of 912 years called after Seth, then by the period of 905 years called after Enos, and so on; but Seth lived contemporaneously with Adam 800 years, Enos with Seth 807 years, and so on. Thus the recorded periods of 8225 years, from Adam to the Flood, have been systematically shortened to 1656 years, for dogmatic reasons.

We maintain that the pre-Noachian period, thus unhistorically shortened, was made to appear historical. This was done by regarding as personal names the names given to periods, by assuming that each patriarch had only one son, and by letting these sons live together with their fathers exactly as many years as were required by the scheme of 7000 years. If the first period of Hebrew chronology had been assumed to have lasted, or had according to tradition lasted, 930 years, and had possibly been called Adam, these 930 years were regarded as the duration of Adam's life; he was recorded to have been 130 years old when he begat Seth, and father and son were stated to have lived together 800 years. Instead of adding together the years of possibly traditional successive periods, those years were added together which represented the ages of each patriarch at the birth of the one recorded son. Thus the 1656 years were obtained, as required by the scheme of 7000 years, which scheme, as we shall now proceed to show, could not have been connected with Hebrew chronology before the time of Ezra.

In the seventieth year after the destruction of the temple by Nebuchadnezzar, 586 B.C., that is in the year 516, the sixth year of Darius Hystaspes, the newly-built temple was finished and consecrated, in exact fulfilment of the prophecy of the seventy years of exile in the book of Jeremiah.

But already in 536, in the fiftieth or jubilee year after the destruction of the temple, Cyrus, the anointed of God, had given permission to the Israelites to return from Babylon to Judæa. The restoration of the theocracy, therefore, took place during the last twenty of the seventy years of Jeremiah. It soon became apparent that this return of a small part of two tribes could only be regarded as a provisional fulfilment of the promised restoration of Israel, gathered from all the countries to which they had been exiled, a mere forerunner of the promised glory of Jerusalem. It became the duty of Israel's spiritual leaders to fan the faint longing of the people after the final restitution of all things. No better means could have been selected for this object than the attempt to fix the times of the end. A symbol was deemed to be necessary, and a symbol was created.

The historical events which had led to the building of the second temple under Zerubbabel were regarded as types of the future fulfilment of prophecy. The seventy periods of Jeremiah were enlarged to seventy jubilee periods, or to 3500 years, seeing that the first jubilee year after the destruction of the temple had marked the commencement of the typical restoration. Naturally the idea thus suggested itself to regard the twenty last years of the now ended period of seventy years—that is, the time from 536 to 516—as a type of the last twenty jubilee periods—that is, of $20 \times 50 = 1000$ years, as a type of the future millennium, which was to close the 7000 years of the earth's existence.

The restoration of Israel, which, after the seventy years of Jeremiah in 516, at the time of the consecration of the second temple, was regarded as future—the Messianic time, when the light of Zion should come—was connected with the last twenty jubilees, that is with a period of a thousand years, commencing with the fiftieth jubilee, with the jubilee of jubilees. The seventy jubilee periods which ended with the millennium were reckoned, like their type, the seventy years of Jeremiah, from the destruction of the temple in 586. The initiated contemporaries of Zerubbabel, of Joshua and Ezra,[1] would know that the millennium, the coming of the expected Messiah, must begin analogously with the typical return under Zerubbabel, with the jubilee of jubilees, or after $50 \times 50 = 2500$ years after 586 B.C., and thus the millennium was placed in the approaching time from 1914–2914 A.D. The required symbol would not have been complete unless the destruction of Babylon, which preceded the typical restoration of the theocracy under Cyrus, was marked as a type of a future fall of Babylon which should precede the millennium. Already the prophet Zechariah speaks of a future fall of Babylon, which is fully described in the Apocalypse. The seer of Patmos expected the millennium in his time, or soon after, and thus proves that he had certainly no knowledge of the unhistorical and unprophetic scheme of the time of Ezra.

The following tables will help to elucidate the above remarks:—

THE SECOND HALF OF THE 7000 YEARS, OR FROM THE DESTRUCTION OF THE FIRST TEMPLE TO THE END OF THE MILLENNIUM, 3500 YEARS.

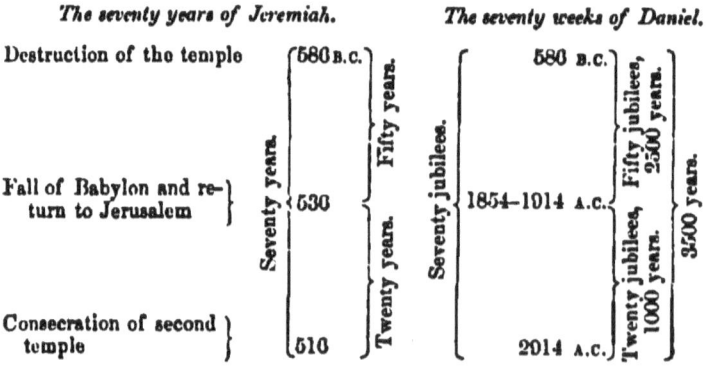

The seventy years of Jeremiah.   *The seventy weeks of Daniel.*

---

[1] About the time of Ezra, see pp. 52–57. 61 - 66.

EZRA AND THE SCRIPTURES.

The First Half of the 7000 Years, or from the Destruction of the First Temple to the Creation of Heaven and Earth, 3500 Years.

From the destruction of the first temple to its foundation, 385 years	586–971 B.C.	
From the foundation of the temple to the exodus from Egypt, 592 years[1]	971–1563 B.C.	
From exodus from Egypt to exodus from Haran, 430 years	1563–1993 B.C.	3500.
From exodus from Haran to the Noachian flood, 367 years	1993–2360 B.C.	
From the Noachian flood to the creation of Adam, 1656 years	2360–4016 B.C.	
From creation of Adam to the creation of heaven and earth, 70 years	4016–4086 B.C.	
Total	. 7000 years.	

This type of the 70 weeks or jubilee periods of the future could not suggest itself before the return from Babylon and the consecration of the temple. Not earlier than from 536–516 B.C. could the historically fulfilled 70 years of Jeremiah be regarded as typical. The scheme of 7000 years, with which the millennium was connected, could only then be conceived in the form shown above, and be suggested by Biblical chronology. We shall see that in the year 515 Ezra's mission to Jerusalem took place, and we may assume that this learned scribe, by whom the Biblical text was revised and settled, did sanction, if he did not suggest, this scheme which has given rise to the theory of the millennium.

From the preceding tables it will be seen that the scheme of 7000 years, intended to be supported by Biblical chronology, requires the shortening to 1656 years of the time intervening between the Flood and the creation of Adam. With the remaining mystic number of seventy years for the seven days of the creation of the universe, this period forms the exact complement of 7000 years. The 1656 expressed years and the 70 implied years clearly prove that the period from

---

[1] According to Josephus, *Ant.* viii. 3, 1; confirmed by St. Paul, Acts xiii. 20. Compare also Judges xi. 26; see p. 27.

the exodus to the foundation of the temple was acknowledged as a period of 592, and not of 480 years. Had this period been fixed in the text at 592 instead of 480 years, to which former duration both St. Paul and Josephus refer, then it would have been more easy to detect the systematic alteration of a part of Hebrew chronology. We cannot, therefore, help surmising that the incorrect limitation of the period from the exodus to the foundation of the temple, like the intentional shortening of the pre-Noachian period to 1656 years, originated in a design.

It corresponds well with the intentional alteration of the most ancient period of recorded Hebrew chronology, that the 1656 years are composed of twenty-three Pleiades periods of seventy-two years, as Mr. R. G. Haliburton, of Nova Scotia, has first discovered.[1]

POSSIBLE ANTEDILUVIAN TRADITION OF 8225 YEARS.

The period of 1656 years, now proved to have been incorrectly determined, may be possibly connected with a very remote tradition. By regarding the periods before the Flood, with which the names of the so-called patriarchs have been connected, as successive periods, the 8225 years before the Flood would reach to the year 10,585 B.C., if the Hebrew year of the Flood was 2360, as we hope to prove to demonstration. It would not follow, however, from this, that in the eleventh millennium before our era the first man saw the light of day.[2]

[1] R. G. Haliburton, *New Materials for the History of Man, derived from a Comparison of the Calendars and Festivals of Nations*, Halifax, Nova Scotia, 1863 and 1864, partly reprinted in Piazzi Smyth's *Life and Work at the Great Pyramid*. Compare our shortly appearing work, *The Pleiades and the Zodiac in their relations to Biblical Symbolism*, dedicated to R. G. Haliburton, who first discovered the connection of the Pleiades with mythology.

[2] See Appendix, Note I.

Sargon II. states that 350 ancestors of his reigned over the Assyrians, and the dates of Ctesias, whose testimony may have been underrated, go far to correct this assertion, as we shall point out. As all chronological periods hitherto known from cuneiform inscriptions will be proved correct, Sargon's assertion may be so likewise. If Berosus in the fourth century before Christ could transmit historical Babylonian dates reaching up to 2458, the Hebrews during the Babylonian captivity could test or correct their traditional chronology by the cuneiform inscriptions, and by the traditions of Chaldæan priests. We shall show that the earliest historical date of Berosus known to us, the capture of Babylon by the 'Medes' in 2458, has been assigned by Hebrew chronology to what in Genesis is called the birth of Shem. We shall moreover show that the commencement of the second Chaldæan dynasty in 1993–1992 with a probable Kudurlagamer, synchronises with the exodus of Abraham from Haran. This connection between Hebrew and Chaldæan chronology, once proved, will permit us to conjecture that if there was a Babylonian or an Assyrian chronological tradition which went beyond 2458, the Hebrews in Babylonia, and therefore Ezra, may have known it.

It becomes an ever-increasing probability that tribal traditions existed in pre-historic times—that long before the invention of any recorded alphabet, the knowledge of a verbal tradition formed the highest privilege of the highest class, to which the priests belonged. If so, the unabbreviated periods of Genesis which precede the record of the Noachian deluge may have been thus preserved by the channels of tradition.[1] Without our

---

[1] We have suggested that the period of Enos the son of Seth, of the Ischita and religious reformer of the Nabathæans (Ish-fire), which would reach to the time from 8743–7838 B.C., may have referred to the reign of the sixth Chavanian Vistaspa in Bactra, and to Zoroaster, in whose time, as in the days of Enos, 'men began to publish the name of Jehova,' the Jahu of the Assyrians or Iranians. After the Bactrian reformer Ishita-Seth-Zoroaster, the first king of the Median dynasty of

assuming this, the historical chronology of the Hebrews can be proved to have commenced, as we are going to show, by the Median capture of Babylon in 2458 B.C.

Hebrew chronology is indeed the greatest marvel of the world, even if we do not admit the possibility that Hebrew tradition goes back to the time of Eden—that is, as we with others maintain,[1] to the earliest traditional sojourn of the Aryan or Japhetic race on the highland of Pamer, near the sources of the Oxus and Indus, in the present Thibet. It is curious that the first date of the most ancient Samaritan tradition transmitted to us is the year 4700 for the creation of the world. This is a purely astronomical date, which refers to the entry of the sun at the vernal equinox into the sign of Taurus. The 4700 years cannot have been inserted into the Samaritan chronology before the year 382 B.C., when the sun entered Pisces at the vernal equinox. To the number 382 thus obtained, the duration of the precession of the equinoctial points for two degrees or two signs, those of Aries and Taurus, has been added. We do not know how this duration was then determined, but taking the mean time between the shortest or the correct date, $2 \times 2158 = 4316 + 382 = 4698$, and the longest date, $2 \times 2160 + 382 = 4702$, we may regard 4700 as referring to this astronomical date. The year of the Samaritan Flood is connected with 4700, and therefore of equally modern date. The Samaritans, wishing to harmonise their chronology with Hebrew chronology, deducted 1656 years from 4700, and thus they obtained 3044 for the year of the Flood. The Hebrew date for what is called the Noachian deluge—that is, as we shall see, the year 2360 B.C.—has

---

Babylon may have received, as reported, the name of Zoroaster, whilst the name of Hystaspes or Vashtaspa would point to the Bactrian king of the Iranians, who may have been one of the 350 Assyrian ancestors of Sargon II.

[1] For this, and for our ethnic interpretation of the birth of Shem, compare the important new work of Professor J. G. Müller in Basel, *Die Semiten in ihrem Verhältniss zu Chamiten und Japhetiten*. 1872.

been determined by the implied Biblical date for the birth of Shem. The recorded catastrophe is placed 98 years after an historical event, designated as the birth of Shem.

'THE BIRTH OF SHEM' IN 2458 B.C.

The starting-point of provably historical chronology, as inserted in the books of Moses, is the birth of Shem, to which Genesis refers, and of which we shall now show that it certainly coincides with the taking of Babylon by the Medes in 2458 B.C. Assuming this for the sake of argument, the Noachian Flood, according to the Mosaic writings, took place in 2360; for, two years after this recorded catastrophe, Shem was a hundred years old.[1] The very same year is referred to by Censorinus, about 238 A.D., who states, on the authority of Varro, 'the most learned of the Romans,' born 116 B.C., that the deluge took place 'about the year 2360.' As we have derived our Flood-date from the above passage in Genesis, this coincidence is not unimportant, and it confirms our date for the birth of Shem, which is implied in Genesis. But every doubt as to the correctness of this date must vanish before the fact that the remarkable results of our chronology, the establishment of all the synchronisms demanded by the Bible and by the Assyrian inscriptions, would not have been attained had we not regarded the year 2458 as the starting-point of the provably historical chronology of the Hebrews.

THE EXODUS FROM HARAN IN 1993-1992 B.C.

Accepting the year 2458 for the birth of Shem, and thus also the year 2360 for the Flood, Abraham left Haran in the year 1993, that is, 367 years after the Flood.

[1] Gen. xi. 10. About the 950 years of Noah, see *The Pleiades and the Zodiac.*

According to a statement of Berosus, a new dynasty came to the throne in Babylon in 1992, as will be seen by our restoration of his Babylonian dynasties. On Abraham's return from Egypt to Canaan, he and his men took part in the defeat of Chedorlaomer, king of Elam, who had invaded Syria or Canaan, according to Genesis. Later cuneiform inscriptions mention a Kudur-Mabuk, 'servant' of (the divinity?) Mabuk, and after another divinity Lagamer, a ruler of Elam, Kudur-Lagamer, may have been set up in Babylon in 1992. After his name the Hebrew name Chedorlaomer is likely to have been formed. The inscriptions call Kudur-Mabuk 'Lord of Elam and Syria,' and the Bible makes similar statements about Chedorlaomer. As it is certain from Genesis that Abraham left Haran and returned from Egypt to Canaan before the defeat of Chedorlaomer in the vale of Shiddim, and that in the year of his leaving Haran a new dynasty came to the throne in Babylon, it is not unreasonable to assume that the Chedorlaomer of the Bible corresponds with the first king of the fourth dynasty, whose name may have been Kudurlagamer.

THE BATTLE OF SHIDDIM IN 1070 B.C.

The Hebrews must have entered Egypt, and commenced the period of their servitude in this country, a few years after the victory over Chedorlaomer and his allies, that is, certainly not later than thirty years after Abraham's leaving Mesopotamia, that is, in 1963, or 400 years before the exodus from Egypt in 1563. Only on this supposition the fact can be explained that in the Mosaic writings the period of Hebrew servitude extended over 430 years according to the one passage, and over 400 years according to the other. St. Paul follows the statement in Exodus, and confirms the explanations in the Greek text, when he dates the 430 years of Hebrew servitude from the exodus from Mesopotamia, and thus extends the servitude to that in Canaan as well as that in Egypt.[1]

Our chronology leads to a remarkable confirmation of this Apostolic statement. The victory of Abraham and his allies over Chedorlaomer and his allies must necessarily have taken place, according to Biblical records, during the thirty years from the exodus from Haran to the commencement of Hebrew servitude in Egypt. As already pointed out, in the selfsame year in which, according to our chronology, Abraham left Haran, 1993–1992, a new dynasty came to the throne in Babylon, the first king of which may now be assumed to have been Kudurlagamer of Elam. It follows that the fourteenth year of his rule, in which the battle of Shiddim occurred, fell in the year 1979, and took place sixteen years before the commencement of the Hebrew servitude in Egypt, which lasted 400 years.

THE PHARAOH OF JOSEPH.

The Pharaoh of Joseph was certainly one of the Hyksos kings, and therefore a successor of Saïtes, whom Manetho names as the first of these kings. The same name, that of Setaapethi-Nubti, occurs in an inscription of Ramesses II., found in Tanis-Avaris, in which it is stated that this Saïtes (not the first of his name) rebuilt Tanis 400 years before Ramesses II., and that he had erected a temple to the god Seth, the national god of the Hyksos. The rebuilding of Tanis-Avaris, that is, of Zoan, the fortress of the Hyksos, seven years before the original foundation of which Hebron was built, falls in the year 1744, if our date for the reign of Ramesses II. can be maintained. Abraham lived in Hebron-Kirjath-Arba before the battle against Chedorlaomer,[2] of which we have proved that it occurred in the year 1979.

[1] Ex. xii. 40, 41; Gal. iii. 17; Heb. xi. 9. Compare Gen. xv. 13, 14 Acts vii. 6, 7.   [2] Gen. xiii. 18; Num. xiii. 22.

The successor of Tiaaken, that is, King Kames of Thebes, the father of Ahmes, is mentioned on the monuments as Tsafento, or 'sustainer or feeder of the world,' a title which corresponds with the Hebrew Zaphnat-Pa'hneach, 'procurer of life,' the title which the Pharaoh gave to Joseph. For this reason Manetho and those who instructed him may have assumed that Joseph lived in the reign of Apepi or Apophis, the last of the Hyksos kings, so called by the Egyptians after the serpent, the symbol of Seth, the god of the shepherds. If our chronology be right, there can be no doubt but that Abraham was received in Egypt by one of the Hyksos-Pharaohs. This is also indirectly confirmed by the facts that Hebron was built seven years before Tanis-Avaris-Zoan, the frontier fortress of the Hyksos, and that Abraham lived in Hebron, as already observed, before the battle of Shiddim in 1979. It follows from this that the fortress of the shepherds existed in the time of Abraham's journey to Egypt, between 1993 and 1979. Finally, the regency of Joseph under a Hyksos-Pharaoh is indirectly confirmed by the statement in Genesis that all the Egyptians said unto Joseph: 'Thou hast saved (sustained) our lives; let us find grace in the sight of my lord, and we will be (the foreign) Pharaoh's servants.'[1] Thus also it is best explained why the Pharaoh of Hebrew bondage, being a native Egyptian (Ahmes), knew nothing of Joseph.

FROM THE DEATH OF JOSEPH TO THE EXODUS.

If we prove that the implied Hebrew date for the exodus from Egypt is 1563, then the hitherto undeterminable period from the death of Joseph to the exodus consisted of 143 years; for, if Terah died in 2138, Abraham lived from 2068-1893; Isaac, from 1968-1788; Jacob

[1] Gen. xlvii. 25.

from 1909-1763. Joseph was born in 1816, sold in 1799, raised to the regency in 1786, and he died in 1706, his father having gone to Egypt *probably about* 1779-1778, *when* 130 *years old*, and in the first year of the famine.

THE PHARAOH OF THE BONDAGE.

According to Manetho, the Pharaoh of Hebrew bondage was called Tuthmoses (Thot-Moses), and the Pharaoh of the exodus Amenophis. Still assuming that the exodus of the Israelites took place in 1563, Amenophis I., that is the successor of Ahmes or Amoses I., the Amasis of Ptolemy's chronology, who also might be called Thot-Moses, can alone have been the Pharaoh of the exodus, according to any possible Egyptian chronology. It is true that a son of the Amenophis of the exodus is called Sethos, according to the Manethonian tradition as transmitted to us; and this name of the Hyksos deity could hardly be given to a prince of the reigning house which had finally expelled them. But this is no counter-argument of any weight, as the information may not have been correct, and as Seth was certainly not long after reinstalled as an Egyptian deity. Again, according to the Manethonian legend, this prince was called Rampses (Ramesses?), and this name, originally one of a deity, actually occurs in an inscription as one of the names or titles of a prince of the family of Ahmes, so that also Amenophis might have had the title Rampses. After this deity, not after Amenophis-Rampses, or another king, the first rallying-point of the Israelites was called Ramses.

The monuments clearly show that Ahmes drove the foreign rulers out of Avaris. An inscription testifies to the fact that Lower Egypt was reconquered from the foreign rulers in the twenty-second year of the rule of Ahmes, the first king of the eighteenth dynasty. An

16   MESOPOTAMIANS FROM THE EAST.

Admiral Ahmes, who served under Ahmes and under his two successors, relates in another inscription that he took part in an attack by land and by water on Tanis-Avaris, the fortress of the Hyksos. Till lately it has remained doubtful whether the Hyksos regained possession of this fortress, and were repulsed a second time, and then finally left Egypt, as the Manethonian legend affirms. We shall try to prove that the Hebrews, called 'the lepers,' were the allies of the Hyksos, and that the exodus of the former took place five years before the final expulsion of the latter from the land of the Nile.

ETHNIC RELATIONS OF THE HEBREWS.

The Hebrews, literally those 'from beyond,' and not necessarily from beyond the Euphrates, were the descendants as well of Abraham, whose ancestors had lived in the Chaldæan Ur, as of the assumed personage Shem, who was born in the year when the Berosian Medes (Iranians) took Babylon in 2458. The ethnic traditions of these Hebrews contained in the tenth chapter of Genesis can be locally traced from the sources of the Oxus and Indus to Mesopotamia, where the first settlements of the Shemites were situated.[1] These facts confirm our suggestion, that the unabbreviated periods of Genesis from 'Adam' to 'the Deluge,' whatever these words may have signified, seem to be based on tribal traditions. According to Genesis, the first inhabitants of Shinar came from the East, and according to Babylonian tradition, 'the mountain of the world' lay to the East. We hold that Japhetites and Hamites (Aryans and Turyans?) came from the East, and long before 'the birth of Shem' in Mesopotamia, became the first historical inhabitants of this country, called Shinar—Babylonia. It is submitted that these

[1] See our map on the Aboriginal Migrations of Mankind in *Einheit der Religionen*, i.

JAPHETITES AND HAMITES BEFORE SHEMITES. 17

Mesopotamians from the East can, according to Genesis, be traced from the far East to the West; that is, to Mesopotamia, the land of Shem's birth and settlements. According to this scheme, the Japhetites and Hamites lived in the East long before the birth of Shem, whilst the Shemites were formed in Mesopotamia by a combination of Indian or Babylonian and Iranian or Assyrian Japhetites and Hamites in 2458 B.C., when 'Medes' took Babylon. The recorded first descendants of Adam lived on the borders of the Gihon-Oxus, in the Hamitic land of Cush, and adjoining the Eden of the second chapter of Genesis, the Aryana-Vaëjo, or Aryan home, the Arivarvi of Tiglat Pilesar, on the north of the Hindu-Cush or Indian Cush.

Without here further entering on the discussion of these questions, we refer to the above facts and the hypothesis based upon them, in order to show the necessary ethnic interpretation of what is in Genesis called the birth of Shem.[1] We hope to establish, by a comparison of the principal flood-stories which have come down to us, that the story of Noah and his three sons cannot be taken literally, and must be figuratively interpreted.[2] It is necessary to refer to this here, inasmuch as it has an important bearing on the now established intentional incorrectness of the period of 1656 years from Adam to the Flood, and because of the equally certain existence of flood-stories more or less similar to that of Genesis, but infinitely more ancient than the year 2360. With the period of 1656 years falls the assumption that the long-lived patriarchs ever existed, though such individuals may possibly have lived during the unabbreviated periods of more than eight thousand years named after them.

[1] This was first suggested by C. Lenormant in 1834. The same result has been independently arrived at, and has been supported with an unsurpassable depth of scientific and impartial criticism in Professor J. G. Müller's work on the Shemites in their relations to Hamites and Japhetites.

[2] *The Pleiades and the Zodiac, in their relations to Biblical Symbolism*, in a work publishing in German, and from which an English edition is being prepared.

We have explained ethnically the birth of Shem, which we shall conclusively prove to coincide with the capture of Babylon by the Medes of Berosus, connected with the Zend-Avesta, or tradition written. We maintain, that after the Aryan separation in the Himalaya, and the conquest of India, referred to in Genesis as Havilah or Chavilah, some Indian Aryans or Japhetites ruling over Non-Aryans (Turyans?) or Hamites, that is, a race of high-caste whites and (broadly speaking) of low-caste blacks, migrated from India to the Persian Gulf, through Arabia to Egypt and Libya, and thence to Canaan. From Sidon they went towards Shinar, probably first so called by the Assyrians, the 'Sumir' of cuneiform inscriptions,[1] a people cognate with the Medes, who ruled there 224 years before Urukh, after the subjugation of the Babylonians, Akkadians, Hamites, or Indians. Thus was realised the recorded prophecy of Noah, that 'Japhet shall dwell in the tents of Shem,' that is, in Mesopotamia, and that Canaan, or Ham, shall be his servant or slave. The Black was the slave of the White long before the time to which the name of Noah is made to refer.

No wonder, then, that on the advance of the Cushite king of Elam, Abraham the Hebrew, the leader of those who had come from beyond, from the East, the leader of Indian Japhetic and Indian Hamitic tribes, immediately broke up from Haran, and went to Egypt to join the foreign or aboriginally Non-Egyptian rulers of that land. We understand why the Hyksos-Pharaoh kindly received Abraham, and why the Hebrews took a leading part, possibly with the direct assistance of the allies of the Egyptians in Canaan, if not of the Egyptians themselves, in the repulsion of the Cushite king of Elam, whose object seems to have been, with the assistance of the Cushites of Africa, of the native Egyptians and Ethio-

[1] M. Lenormant's unpublished discovery, who refers to W. A. I. ii. 46, 1, second column, for the word Sumirituv, promising to prove that Sumir = Asshur, and also = Sungir (Singara = Sinar). The positive proof for the latter derivation, first suggested by Dr. Haigh, is found by M. Lenormant in Aboulfaradj (*Hist. Dynast.* p. 18): 'Shennaar, which is El-Samarrah.'

pians, to drive the Hyksos from Egypt, with their upper-caste Iranian-Japhetic or Iranian-white rulers. With the assistance of an Indian Japhetite or white ruler, of a Chaldæan (Chaldi or Celt?), this probable object of Chedorlaomer was averted, and it was left to Ahmes and Amenophis to carry it out more than 400 years later; after that, 'without cause, the Assyrians,' more correctly the Iranians, the Hyksos, had oppressed 'the stranger,' the people of God, the Hebrews, their allies in Egypt.[1]

We shall now point out the possible ethnic relations between the Medes of Berosus, who ruled in Babylon from 2458 to 2234, and the Hyksos, who possessed Egypt soon after 2234, and the Arabians, who ruled in Babylon from 1534-1289. For the most important questions now arise, Whence came and what can have become of the mighty host of the Hyksos who ruled Egypt for so many centuries?

We regard the Hyksos as ethnically connected and even probably identical with the Mesopotamian Medes, who in the year 2234, according to Berosus, were expelled from Babylon after having reigned there since 2458. We have seen that the Hyksos-fortress Tanis-Avaris-Zoan was (originally?) built an indeterminable time before the battle of Shiddim, 1979, which was fought 255 years after, in 2234. Our chronology shows an approximate synchronism between the expulsion of the Berosian Medes from Babylon by Urukh in 2234, and the conquest of Egypt by the Hyksos, probably before 2069 B.C., to which time the 511 years of Manetho would reach. Moreover, both Medes and Hyksos had the serpent symbol. On the other hand, another important and at least debatable probability results from our chronology, that is, the identity of the Hyksos expelled from Egypt with the Arabian or Canaanite dynasty of Berosus in Babylon.

According to our restoration of the Babylonian dynasties, these Arabians, or Canaanites as the Nabathæans call them, began their rule in Babylon in 1534 with Hammurabi, who

[1] Is. lii. 4.

is thus proved, in literal harmony with a cuneiform inscription, to have commenced his reign exactly 700 years after Urukh, now proved to have been the first of the eleven kings which, according to Berosus, began to rule in 2234. This Hammurabi was the immediate successor of the Queen Ellat-Gula, of the dynasty of Sargon I.; he is designated as a stranger, and his accession to the throne, as fixed by us in 1534, took place but twenty-four years after the date of Orosius for the death of the last Hyksos-Pharaoh, in 1558. Berosus may have had reasons for calling this dynasty an Arabian one, if the Hyksos could be (broadly) called Assyrians, as Isaiah seems to do.

Hammurabi, as a Hyksos and Mede, might be called king or chief of 'the Cassi' (Cossaei). His name has been connected with the Assyrian Ammu, the sun, though others consider it Cushite, like the names of his successors. Even on this probably correct hypothesis, the five hundred and more years which the Hyksos spent in the land of Cush, in Egypt, would suffice to bring about a preponderance of the Non-Aryan over the Aryan element, a preponderance of Akkadians or 'highlanders.'

Like the so-called Shemites of the Bible, the Hyksos, whose kings according to the monuments were certainly of Aryan descent, migrated from Aryan into Non-Aryan, Hamitic, or Cushite districts, where their Aryan language became in course of time more or less Cushite. Thus the Babylonians as well as the Medes, the Madai of Genesis, may have originally been ethnically comprised under the name of Chaldæans, Kaldi (Celts, Aryans, or Japhetites), the Assyrian (or Syrian?) Rotennu-Kaldu of the Ebers-inscription. The priests belonged to the upper castes, and in Wales and Iona are called Kaldi.

Thus the way may be opened for the removal of two objections to our theory:—

1. That the language of the upper classes and priests of ancient Babylonia, the so-called Akkadians, was agglutinative and allied to that of Finns and Tartars;

2. That the Kaldi are first met with as a small tribe on the Persian Gulf in the eighth century B.C., whence they moved slowly northward, and at length, under Merodach Baladan, possessed themselves of Babylon.

It is by no means certain that the first historical inhabitants of Shinar-Babylonia, who had come from the East, and built Babylon before the 'Medes' took it in 2458, were not Chaldæans in the above sense of the word, that is, combined upper-caste Aryans and low-caste Non-Aryans or Cushites. Again, the post-Median dynasty of Urukh may have been a Chaldæan dynasty, as the Egyptians knew the Kaldu in the 16th century.

Synchronous history shows that there were Kassi in Elam-Babylonia. The Egyptian Cushites, as well as the Kassi of Elam, we connect with 'the land of Cush,' watered by the Gihon-Jichoon-Amu-Oxus, and thus with the home of the Aryans, whose features the Hyksos are on monuments represented to have had. The deity of Hammurabi, king of Cushites, was Maruduk or Merodach, which name, as we shall see, has lately been connected with Nimrod 'the son of Cush.' As Aryans were in the East rulers of Turyans (Cushites?), so in the West they ruled over Cushites. As the Bible seems to call the Hyksos 'Assyrians,' so Herodotus calls the Assyrians under Sennacherib 'Arabians.' We identify the expelled Hyksos with the 'Arabians' of Berosus, distinguishing from them the 'Chara' or 'Chal,' who, according to the Harris-papyrus, established a foreign rule before Ramesses III.[1]

If the allies of the Israelites in Egypt, the Hyksos, whom Tacitus represents as ethnically connected, and Josephus as identical, with the Israelites, ruled in Babylon eleven years before the death of Moses, then we can hardly help surmising that this Hyksos-rule in Babylon was more or less directly connected with the advance of the Israelites under Joshua from Shiddim, with the conquest of Canaan, and with the division of the land in 1518. Othniel may

[1] Herod. ii. 141. Mr. Cooper connects Chalu with Chul (Hul), son of Aram.

have put an end to the short dominion of Chusan-Risathaim, the Cushite, under the indirect influence of the Hyksos in Babylon.

The Hyksos-rule in Egypt, perhaps beginning soon after 2234, and ending in 1558 B.C., lay between two rules of possibly the same people, of the Medes in Babylon from 2458–2234 B.C., and their second rule 700 years later, in the same city, as the 'Arabians' of Berosus, from 1534–1289 B.C. The capture of Babylon by the Medes is in Genesis shown to synchronise with what is there called the birth of Shem. Interpreting ethnically this event, we may say: When the Mede entered Babylon, Shem was born, that is, Japhet (the Aryan) dwelt in the tents of Shem, or in Mesopotamia, where Canaan (Ham, broadly the Turyan) was his servant. From 2458–1289 B.C., or for 1,169 years, the Hebrew seems to have been the ally of one and the same nation of the 'Medes' in Babylon, of the 'Hyksos' in Egypt, and of the 'Arabians' in Babylon. Hebrew tradition is Indian-Iranian.

We may now suggest, that the presumable upper castes of the Hyksos, and the possible upper castes of the Hebrews, to which Abraham would have belonged, represented the non-Hamitic or Japhetic, the Aryan element, as this is certainly implied by the representations of the Hyksos on monuments found at Avaris.[1] Assuming this with regard to the Hebrews, no kind of race-distinction existed between the Hyksos-Pharaoh and Abraham, to whom he gave a friendly reception, nor between Joseph and the Pharaoh who made him regent. The Japhetic or Aryan element formed the link between all the various descendants of the Indians and of the Iranians, and thus between the Babylonians, Medes, and Assyrians. The probability gains ground, that Indian Japhetites, more and more overwhelmed by the Hamitic element, constituted the aboriginal Egyptian (not African) nation, as well as the first historical nation on the Euphrates,

[1] Compare Pleyte, *Religion des Préisraélites.*

the Babylonians, who, according to Genesis, broke up or journeyed from the East, and came unto Shinar-Babylonia. When the Medo-Iranians of Berosus, Hamites ruled by Japhetites, followed their Indian brethren to Mesopotamia, and took Babylon in 2458, the Japhetite element received a fresh and powerful impetus, which must have been very welcome to the high-caste Babylonians, as well as to the Hebrews, who had lived among the Chaldæans. The Medes from the Caspian, whose first king is said to have been called Zoroaster, after the great Monotheist, were the people of the Zendavesta. If in this book no so-called Semitic ideas or words are traceable, this is because its tradition is older than the 'birth' of Shem, the capture of Babylon by the Medes in 2458 B.C.

We regard Abraham, the Hebrew chief, as an Aryan or Japhetite, whose ancestors had lived among those Chaldæans who had first come to Shinar from the East, that is, from India, and we regard the Hyksos as belonging to some specific tribes of their Medo-Iranian brethren, whose ancestors had lived, together with the forefathers of the Babylonians, in the north of the Himalaya until the Aryan separation which led to the conquest of India. On the advance of the Cushite Chedorlaomer, who may have been allied with Ethiopia, Abraham, as representative of the non-Hamitic, or Japhetic element, and of the tradition entrusted to the same, would on this ground alone have had ample reason for his journey to Egypt, where the Hyksos welcomed the Aryan leader.

On the not improbable assumption, that there were at this time in or near Mesopotamia Assyrians independent from and only ethnically connected with the Medes of the first historical dynasty of Berosus, Chedorlaomer probably made the Assyrians tributary, since these are neither mentioned as the allies of the king of Elam or of those kings who opposed him. This distinction already referred to between the Assyrians proper and the Medes and Hyksos can be confirmed by several facts. We are told in Genesis, according to one of the two possible readings of the passage, that from the land of Shinar 'went forth Ashur and built Nineveh.' Assuming the name Ashur to refer to the Assyrians, they may have been raised to political importance by the expulsion of the Medes from Babylon. Manetho gives us the important information, that the first Hyksos-king in Avaris was afraid of the growing power of the Assyrians. Thus the commencement of Hyksos-rule and of Assyrian rule is made to synchronise. Nineveh might have been built by this Ashur of Genesis, and perhaps already soon after 2234, which date, as we shall see, very nearly harmonises with the dates of Ctesias for the foundation of Assyrian power. Herodotus states, that 'the Medes were called anciently by all people Aryans, but when Medea the Colchian came to them from Athens they changed their name.' The Colchians were Cushites or Non-Aryans. Thus our explanation of Medes as Non-Aryans ruled by Aryans is confirmed.

We therefore come to the following ethnic results. The Hyksos, later called Arabians, were Medes, politically distinct from the Assyrians, but ethnically connected with them as Iranians. The Babylonians, with whom the Abrahamitic Hebrews were ethnically connected, were descendants from the combined (mixed?) Japhetic and Hamitic Indians. The stranger in Israel was the Iranian. It is a confirmation of this, that the possibly Assyrian divinity Jahu, Jah, Jehova, which Moses first proclaimed among the Hebrews, had not been known to the Hebrew forefathers, as we are expressly told in the Mosaic writings. On the other hand, the Babylonian divinity El we have reason to regard as identical with the El, Eljon, and Elohim of the Hebrews in Abraham's time.[1] Like the Babylonians, the Hebrews are Indians who came from the East to Shinar, where Iranian Medes joined them.

[1] Compare Schrader's *Keilinschriften*, who however holds that the Jehovistic Hamathites may nevertheless have received the name of Jehova through the Hebrews—that is, the descendants of Abraham—as the only representatives of pure Monotheism, though Genesis refers to the proclamation of

THE EXODUS FROM EGYPT IN 1563 B.C.

According to the Spanish presbyter Orosius, born towards the end of the fourth century, who was long in Africa, the Pharaoh of the exodus died 805 years before the foundation of Rome, that is, in the year 1558–1557.[1] Accepting this date and our year for the exodus, 1563, the Amenophis of Manetho would have died five years after this event. This coincidence of Hebrew, Egyptian, and African tradition is remarkable.

According to the Manethonian tradition, the Israelites lived in the fortress of Avaris after the expulsion of the Hyksos from that stronghold, they recalled the Hyksos from Jerusalem, these re-entered Avaris, and from thence ruled thirteen more years over Egypt. Assuming that the Tuthmoses of Manetho refers to Ahmes, and his Amenophis of the exodus to his successor Amenophis I., it is at least curious that Amenophis is stated to have reigned thirteen years, or as long as the final rule of the Hyksos lasted. We are thus led to assume that Amenophis, with the assistance of the Ethiopians, succeeded in recapturing Avaris, and that he pursued the enemy beyond the Syrian border. Now this is what the monuments seem to imply

Jehova in the days of Seth. We have pointed out that the Jehovistic part of the Mosaic writings seems to refer to Iranian (Assyrian), and the Elohistic to Indian (Babylonian) tradition. Also, that the Jehovistic non-Hebrews, Melchizedek and Jethro, point to a pure pre-Abrahamitic Monotheism. The Jehovistic 'strangers,' the Rechabites, seem to be ethnically connected by the genealogies with David, Jethro, and Melchizedek. The identity, now incontrovertibly established, of the Babylonian divinity El with the Assyrian divinity Jahu, with which the El and the Jah-Jehova of the Hebrews respectively correspond, seems to confirm our suggestions. See our *Keys of St. Peter*, the first attempt ethnically to explain 'the stranger' in Israel. About Eljon (El-On) and Jao, see *The Pleiades and the Zodiac*.

Mr. Sayce thinks that the belief that Jahu is found in Assyrian must be given up. Nowhere in the copious lists of gods is the name mentioned, and the proper name which was supposed to contain the divine name begins really with il-ya, 'my God.' But Jlubihd is substituted for Jahubihd.

[1] Oros. i. 10. The name Bokhoris (Hawk-Horus) may be a title which, as by Lysimachus, was given to the last Pharaoh by Orosius.

when they state that Amenophis I. did expel northern people exactly from this part of the country.

Thus a double attack on Avaris seems to be attested, one under Ahmes and one under Amenophis I. After the first and perhaps but partially successful attack on Avaris, the Israelites, the lepers of Manetho, could enter into Avaris, even on the assumption that the Hebrews had not previously been the allies of the Hyksos, and that they were entirely separated from the Hyksos forces, as the Manethonian legend would imply. Friendly Canaanites might even in that case have secured them an important support until the Hyksos returned to Avaris. Five years before this final expulsion of the Hyksos from Avaris and Egypt, and thus in the eighth year of Amenophis I., 1563, the exodus of the Israelites took place, according to Hebrew chronology, as we shall proceed to prove. It would be easy for the Israelites to move unopposed from Avaris to Rameses, whilst the Hyksos had become repossessed of Avaris, into which fortress the Hebrews had been able to enter, after the first attack of the Egyptians. They cannot possibly have been sent there by the Egyptians. Before Amenophis, who may have been at some distance, if not in Ethiopia, could hear that the Hebrews had fled, and before he could reach them with his army, these had already reached the Red Sea.

The connection between the years 1563 and 1558 cannot be regarded as a mere casual coincidence. Accepting these dates, Amenophis I. reigned from 1571–1558, and Tuthmoses III. from 1515–1537. The year 1515 has been independently determined by an astronomical calculation as the first year of Tuthmoses III.[1] The forty-three years between 1515 and 1558 correspond with the Manethonian regnal years between Tuthmoses III. and Amenophis I. The Hebrew year for the exodus, 1563, falls within the reign of this Pharaoh, whose death, like that of the Pharaoh of the exodus, according to Orosius, occurred in 1558.

[1] See Mr. Basil Cooper's essay in the Appendix, Note IV.

THE PERIOD OF 592 YEARS. 27

It is only by accepting our date of 1563 as the implied Biblical date for the exodus, not as an approximate but as a positive one, and by the aid of the restored period of Genesis from the exodus to the foundation of the temple, therefore by accepting the 592 instead of the 480 years, that the Bible-record can for the first time be proved chronologically correct, which asserts that during the end of Solomon's life Jeroboam 'fled into Egypt unto Shishak king of Egypt, and was in Egypt until the death of Solomon.'[1] Again, the implied Hebrew date for the exodus must be 1563, and 592 years later, in 971, the temple must have been founded, if the history of the Book of Judges with its chronological periods is to be confirmed as historical, and if the period of about 300 years, which Jephtha is recorded to have referred to as elapsed from the division of the land under Joshua until Jephtha's time, is to be maintained as approximatively correct. It will be seen that by these facts and arguments we propose to support the implied Biblical date of the exodus, 1563, by the implied correct duration of the Biblical period from the exodus to the foundation of the temple, that is, 592 and not 480 years. We have already given a reason for the hypothesis that the former date is the correct one; we now do not hesitate to assert that we shall raise that hypothesis to the dignity of a fact. Thus we shall prove that the Apostolic limitation of the period from the division of the land until Samuel to 450 years is correct, and that it corrects the Biblical period of 480 years from the exodus to the Temple-foundation. Holy writ corrected by holy tradition.

The second Hebrew period, which together with that of 1656 years is incorrect, as we have seen, is indicated in the Second Book of Kings, according to which there is an interval of only 480 years between the exodus and the foundation of the temple. St. Paul and Josephus correct this mistake. According to the statement of St. Paul,

[1] 1 Kings xi. 40; comp. p. 50.

450 years must be reckoned from the division of the land to Samuel. Accepting the year 1563 for the exodus, St. Paul's period extends from 1518 to 1068. If we add the forty years from the exodus to the death of Moses, and the five years from his death to the division of the land, this already makes 495 years. To these we must add, counting backwards from the foundation of the temple, the three first years of Solomon, the forty years of David, and the twenty-two of Saul, so that, including the thirty-two years of Samuel's judgeship, the duration of which was hitherto not known, the period from the exodus to the foundation of the temple amounts to 592 years. Moreover Josephus not only confirms St. Paul's statement with regard to the 450 years, but also indirectly asserts that Samuel was judge for thirty-two years, inasmuch as he assigns 592 years to the period from the exodus to the foundation of the temple, and 612 to the dedication.[1]

Every doubt as to the correctness of this period, lengthened directly by Josephus and indirectly by St. Paul from 480 to 592 years, must vanish before the light of the following facts. All the dates which the Book of Judges and the First Book of Samuel assign to this time may be consecutively arranged by accepting St. Paul's period of 450 years, which forms the centre of the 592 years, thus clearly demonstrating their historical exactness. The remaining twenty-eight years fill up the gaps occupied by the undetermined rule of Mesopotamia and the interval between the death of Ehud and Barak, for the latter of which twenty years remain, if we restrict the former to eight.

The period of 592 years, as already stated, is implied in a passage of the Book of Judges which no system of

---

[1] *Jos. con. Ap.* ii. 2. By substituting the forty years assigned to Saul in the Acts for the restored text of 1 Sam. xiii. 1, according to which he reigned twenty-two years, Samuel would have been judge only fourteen years instead of thirty-two years. This at least would be highly improbable, but possible according to our chronology.

chronology has hitherto been able to take into consideration.[1] Our chronology alone shows that the Bible is right in reckoning 300 years in round numbers from Jephtha's judgeship to the division of the land under Joshua, 319 years being the exact interval. The chronology of the Book of Judges has been hitherto regarded as at least partly unhistorical, because its periods could not be placed within the frame of 480 years. Accepting 592 years, Solomon and Shishak are contemporaries in harmony with the Bible and monuments, as we shall later point out.

A further confirmation of our year 1563 for the exodus, and of the year 971-970 for the foundation of Solomon's Temple, may be found in the fragmentary Tyrian annals which Josephus borrowed from Menander, according to which Carthage was founded 155 years and eight months after 'the reign of Hiram.' Cicero informs us that the foundation of Carthage took place thirty-nine years before the first Olympiad, *i.e.* 815 B.C.; Hiram must therefore have been king of Tyre 155 years and eight months before this date, *i.e.* 971-970. Since the building of Solomon's Temple began in this year, according to our chronology, the exact coincidence which follows, and which cannot be casual, proves Josephus to be wrong in his further statement, which he cannot have extracted from the Tyrian annals, that the building of the temple was begun in the twelfth, instead of the first year of Hiram.[2]

Finally, our year 1563 for the exodus, and 934 for the death of Solomon, is confirmed by the fact that from the year 934 to 621, which we shall prove to be the twenty-first year of Josiah and the fifth year of Nabopalassar, known by the Ptolemaic reckoning of the eclipse of the moon, there is an interval of 313 years, the exact number required by

---

[1] Judges xi. 26.
[2] *Jos. con. Ap.* i. 18; *Cic. de Rep.* ii. 23. According to Syncellus (§ 310) Troy fell 133 years before Carthage was founded, therefore in 948, in the time of Solomon.

the Bible. This sum total of years is attained by assuming contemporary reigns where they seem to be required, and by thus doing away with the two interregnums hitherto assumed; also by following generally the rule noted in the Mishna, according to which the years of a king's reign ended with New Year's day, so that the first year of his successor's reign need only have lasted a few months, weeks, or days.[1]

RETROSPECT OF CHRONOLOGICAL RESULTS.

Having discovered the year 2458 for the birth of Shem, ethnically explained, as the starting-point of Hebrew chronology, we proceeded to follow the testimony of the Bible to establish the year 1563 for the exodus. Starting from this year, the statements of St. Paul and of Josephus necessarily fixed the year 974 for Solomon's accession to the throne. Again, starting from the eclipse of the moon in the year 621, the fifth year of Nabopalassar, and following the rule of the Mishna, we reckoned backwards, and obtained for the accession of the third king of Israel exactly the same year 974.

This harmony, which it is impossible to ascribe to mere chance, establishes three facts. First, the correctness of our assertion that the birth of Shem, which took place, according to Genesis, ninety-eight years before the Noachian Deluge, coincides with the capture of Babylon by the Medes, according to Berosus in the year 2458. Secondly, the absolute necessity of reckoning 592 years with St. Paul and Josephus, instead of 480, from the exodus to the building of the temple. Finally, that the Mishna-rule was often, but not invariably, followed by Hebrew chroniclers, and that the system of co-regencies adopted by us is correct.

---

[1] Compare Rosch Haschanah. S. Sharpe applied this key in his *Chronology of the Bible*; see our Appendix, Notes 2 and 3.

Each of these three important facts has been left in obscurity by the Bible, either purposely or by accident, and they could have been known only to the initiated. Now, the existence of a secret tradition in Israel, which led to that concealment in the Bible, and to which Justin Martyr directly refers, might be proved by the fact alone, that the statements of St. Paul and of Josephus with regard to the 450 and the 592 years, independently made and yet completely confirming each other, were deduced from one and the same non-written source of knowledge. Both St. Paul and Josephus perceived the error in the First Book of Kings with regard to the 480 years. They completed and corrected Holy Writ by Holy Tradition.

Our Table on the unhistorical scheme of 7000 years, so skilfully veiled over by the initiated, proves to demonstration that the 480 years were devised, because the right number of 592 years would at once have cleared up the designed alteration. For it is only by accepting this interval of 592 years between the exodus and the foundation of the temple, that the 1656 years and the mysterious number of seventy years remain, the latter for the period from the beginning of the Creation to the creation of Adam. It is therefore no chance mistake of a copyist that has crept into the First Book of Kings; but here, as in the case of the 1656 years from Adam to Noah, we have to deal with a design.

How seldom such chronological errors occur in the Old Testament is shown not only by the above-mentioned synchronisms of various countries, but also from the contemporary history of the Assyrians and Israelites, hitherto unreconciled, though required by the Bible and the inscriptions. From the chronology of the Hebrews, as restored in the above manner, follows the satisfactory result, that the contemporary reigns of kings of Israel and Judah with kings of Assyria, Babylonia, and Egypt, as required by the Bible, can all be reconciled.

THE ASSYRIAN ANNALS.

Like the Athenian Archons and the Lacedemonian Ephors, the highest functionaries of Assyria were for the time of one year honoured with a special mark of distinction, viz., that every year was marked in the official lists by the name of one of these functionaries, excepting that the first year of a reign was often marked by a king's name. These official lists contain only rows of names which are from time to time interrupted by horizontal lines of division intended to indicate the accession of a new king. As a rule, in the time before Tiglat Pilesar II., the name of the new king stood next before the line as first Eponym.[1]

According to Mr. G. Smith, of the British Museum, the following are the points of contact hitherto discovered between the Assyrian annals, and the succession of the kings of Babylon, with the duration of their reigns as stated by Claudius Ptolemæus, who flourished between 130 and 161 A.D., and connected them with astronomical calculations which have since been confirmed.

'CANON OF PTOLEMY.'		ASSYRIAN ANNALS.	
Nabonassar	747		
		Tiglat Pilesar	745
Nadius	733		
Kinzirus	731	Kinzirus	731
Elulæus	726	Salmanassar	727
Mardok Empados	721	Sargon	722
Arkaianos	709	Sargon	710
—	704	Sennacherib	705
Bolibus	702	Bel-ibni	703
Aparanadius	699	Assurnadinsum	700
.	.	.	.
Asaridanus	680	Assurahiddin	681
Saosduchinus	667	Saul-mugina	668
Kineladanus	647	Sir-inadin-pal	648

---

[1] Lepsius, *Die Assyrischen Eponymen*, § 33.

ASSYRIAN AND HEBREW SYNCHRONISMS.

The earliest Hebrew-Assyrian synchronism required by the Assyrian annals is connected with a campaign of Shalmaneser II., against Benhadad of Damascus and his confederates, among whom was Ahab of Israel, 'Ahaabbu Sirlai,' which led to the battle of Karkar on the Orontes, in 854. Again, there was a second campaign against Benhadad's successor, Hasael, and a few years later another against Jehu of Israel. According to the official lists, Shalmanezer II. reigned from 859–823, and according to our chronology Ahab reigned from 875–854, and Jehu from 847–819, the former being contemporary with Shalmaneser for five, the latter for twenty-four years. Ahab was killed at the battle of Ramoth-Gilead in the year of the battle of Karkar.

The Septuagint is right in implying that more than one year elapsed between Solomon's death and Rehoboam's intended coronation at Shechem. According to the Assyrian date for the battle on the Orontes against Ahab, we suggest that the first year of Ahab coincided with the first of Jehoshaphat, whilst the fourth of Ahab refers to the first year of Jehoshaphat's sole regency.[1]

The first synchronism which the Bible requires is that of king Menahem of Israel with king Pul of Assyria, whom the former made tributary. Although Eusebius maintains that Pul was mentioned by Berosus as king, yet the name of Pul as belonging to a king has not hitherto been found in Assyrian annals. On the other hand, the Assyrian inscriptions are supposed to represent Menahem as having paid tribute to Tiglat Pilesar. In the First Book of Chronicles Pul is mentioned together with Tiglat Pilesar, and before him, and Tiglat Pilesar is said to have led into captivity the Reubenites, the Gadites, and the half-tribe of Manasseh. The Bible asserts that Pul was also

---
[1] See App. Notes II. and III.

called by God to punish Israel, that the spirit of Pul was stirred up by the God of Israel, and that Menahem was compelled to pay him tribute.[1]

According to our chronology, Menahem reigned from 760 to 750, and, according to the official lists, Tiglat Pilesar reigned from 745 to 727. We are expressly told that the tribute imposed on Menahem (possibly by Pul before Tiglat Pilesar's accession) was not collected and received before the eighth year of Tiglat Pilesar's reign, 738. If, then, we can show that the Pul of the Bible seems to have come to the throne in 763, a few years before Menahem's accession, the assumption will recommend itself, that the tribute imposed by Pul was paid to Tiglat Pilesar.

One of Tiglat Pilesar's predecessors, if there was more than one, may have been called Pul, and Assyria may have made an expedition against Syria before Tiglat Pilesar's accession to the throne. According to the official lists, there was a 'disturbance in the city of Assur' in the year 763, or eighteen years before Tiglat Pilesar, and the statement of this event in the year 763 is preceded on one of the existing copies of these Assyrian chronological tables by a horizontal line of division, which might indicate a change of reign or dynasty. Such a change may in fact be easily reconciled with the disturbance in the capital mentioned about this time. Further, in the year 754, *i.e.* the sixth year of Menahem, and nine years before Tiglat Pilesar, there is a notice of an 'expedition to Arpad,' therefore to Syria, which was probably allied with Israel, though it soon after became the ally of Tiglat Pilesar and Judah. Moreover, the expedition was directed against one of those cities, probably in the neighbourhood of Hamath and the Orontes, to which Sennacherib refers in Isaiah as to cities overthrown by Assyria.[2]

At the time, then, of Menahem's reign in Israel, there

[1] 1 Chron. v. 26. Compare 2 Kings xv. 19–22.
[2] Is. x. 0; xxxvi. 19; xxxvii. 13. Compare 2 Kings xviii. 34; xix. 13.

was an Assyrian expedition to Syria, during which the king of Israel could be compelled to pay tribute, as is asserted by the Bible to have been the case during the reigns of Menahem in Israel and Pul in Assyria. This expedition may have taken place in the reign of Pul, when Menahem did not at once pay, but promised and probably guaranteed by hostages, the payment of tribute mentioned in the Bible, which he had first to collect from 'the mighty men of wealth.' It seems to have been customary to allow some time for the collection of the tribute. This can be proved with regard to the tribute imposed on Aramæan cities by Tiglat Pilesar in 739-738, on which occasion 'the tribute of Menahem of Samaria' was paid together with that of other princes, from which it does not follow that Menahem was then alive. Again, it is stated that Hezekiah was allowed to send by an ambassador the tribute imposed on him by Sennacherib, of whose father and predecessor, Sargon, Mr. Sayce has proved that he imposed tribute on Hezekiah not at Lakish but at Jerusalem. It was probably the refusal to pay this tribute after Sargon's death which led to Sennacherib's invasion, which has been mixed up with that of Sargon. According to Sennacherib's inscription, he took to Nineveh Hezekiah's 'precious molten metal.' This must have included 'all the silver that was found in the house of the Lord and in the treasures of the king's house,' as well as 'the gold from the doors of the temple of the Lord and from the pillars' which Hezekiah had overlaid and now cut off and 'gave' (not sent) to the king of Assyria.[1] Also Manasseh's tribute may have been sent to Nineveh.

We assume for the present that the horizontal line marked on one of the existing copies of official lists does not refer exceptionally to the eclipse of the sun in that year, but signifies, as usual, the change of a king in the year of the disturbance in the city of Assur, 763, and that it refers

[1] Compare 2 Kings xviii. 13-16 with the inscr. Rawl. xii. 18-32.

to the accession of Pul to the throne. Accordingly Pul began his reign three years before Menahem, and, moreover, as the first king of a new dynasty, that is, as we shall show, of the second Assyrian dynasty of Berosus. Accepting this as correct, the first conquest of Babylon by the Assyrians must have taken place, according to the authority of Berosus, 526 years before, *i.e.* in the year 1289 B.C. Now this year, according to a statement of Sennacherib, was in fact the year of the first capture of Babylon. He declares in an inscription that this conquest by the Assyrians took place 600 years before his capture of Babylon, which Mr. Smith places in the year 689.[1] Adding 600 to 689, we gain the above year 1289 for the foundation of the Assyrian monarchy in Babylon.

It is impossible to regard this as a mere chance-coincidence, and still less so since the above event, according to the fragments of the Ptolemæan Canon known to us, falls between the period from 699 to 680, between Aparanadius and Asaredanus, the events of which time cannot at present be determined, either by the Babylonian or by the Assyrian annals. If the year 689 is thus confirmed to be the year of Sennacherib's capture of Babylon, and consequently if that year must be regarded as the starting-point for the 600 years of Sennacherib's inscription, then it is hereby demonstrated that the first Assyrian dynasty, the sixth of Berosus, came to the throne in 1289, and that it was followed, on the authority of the Chaldæan historian, 526 years later, that is, in 763, by the second Assyrian dynasty.

We have, therefore, every reason to expect that further excavations in Nineveh or in Babylon will bring to light additional facts which will fill up the gaps in the Babylonian and Assyrian annals in such a manner as to confirm our positive assertion that in the year 763, in the year of the solar eclipse, a new king, and with him a new dynasty, came to the throne in Babylon.

[1] Berlin *Zeitschrift* of March 1870.

THE PERIOD OF SEVEN HUNDRED YEARS. 37

If, therefore, a king called Pul, or by a composite name in which Pul occurs, or if one of Pul's possible but hardly probable predecessors came to the throne in Babylon in 763, as first king of a new dynasty, then the second Assyrian dynasty, the duration of which could hitherto not be determined, has reigned 138 years, or from 763 to 625, the first year of Nabopalassar. Having absolutely fixed the commencement of the first Assyrian dynasty in 1289, by accepting the 526 years which Berosus assigns to its reign, we may now assert, without fear of contradiction, that the preceding Arabian dynasty of Berosus in Babylon came to the throne in 1534, that is, 245 years before the first Assyrian capture of Babylon.

It is not a little remarkable, that whereas our chronology, in connection with the known dates of Berosus, has confirmed the inscription of Sennacherib about the 600 years between the two captures of Babylon by the Assyrians, another cuneiform inscription containing a date should be confirmed by the same combination, and should thereby absolutely fix the date of Urukh, the builder of the tower of Babel.

The broken cylinder of Nabonadius[1] contains a statement, according to which in his time (555–538 B.C.) there existed in a tower a cylinder of Hammurabi, with the assertion that the tower had been founded 700 years before Hammurabi. This tower can, by the inscriptions, be proved to have been the tower or house, or 'house of Bel,' which Urukh is repeatedly stated to have built at Babel. Accordingly there seem to have been 700 years between Urukh and Hammurabi. Now, as Hammurabi was the first king of a foreign race, who followed at Babylon Queen Ellat-Gula of the House of Sargon I., and as it is now proved that a new dynasty, the Arabian dynasty of Berosus, came to the throne in 1534, the 700 years of Hammurabi's inscription would reach to 2234. This is the precise date for the accession of

[1] See Mr. G. Smith in *Journal of Biblical Archæology*, i. 30, 71.

the first of the eleven kings at Babylon, according to Berosus. It may, therefore, now be asserted, that Urukh was the first king of that post-Median dynasty, and that Hammurabi, the first king of the new dynasty which followed the reign of Ellat-Gula, was the first king of the Arabian dynasty, and that he began his reign in 1534. We have come to this conclusion about the Arabian dynasty of Berosus by commencing the reign of the second Assyrian dynasty with the year 763. Reckoning backwards from this date the 526 years which Berosus assigns to the first Assyrian dynasty, we fixed the commencement of its reign in the year 1289, and reckoning back from this year the 245 years of the Arabian dynasty, we gained the year 1534 for its accession.

Thus, starting from our date for the accession of the second Assyrian dynasty in 763, and reckoning backwards, the dates of Berosus for the reigns of the first Assyrian and the Arabian dynasties led us to the year 1534. We arrive at the same date, if, starting from the date of Berosus for the accession of the post-Median dynasty, that is, from 2234, we allow the 458 years of Berosus for the second Chaldæan dynasty, and if, following the inscription of Hammurabi about the 700 years between him and Urukh, we determine the duration of the reigns of the post-Median dynasty by 242 years. Thus the 458 and the 242 years fill up the interval of 700 years which Hammurabi's inscription with marvellous accuracy demands. The correctness of this earliest date on cuneiform inscriptions is proved beyond all doubt by the now established fact that Hammurabi began to reign $245 + 526 = 771$ years before 763, the accession of the second Assyrian dynasty.

These remarkable conclusions are directly connected with our assumed date of 763 for the accession of the second Assyrian dynasty in Babylon, of which the first or one of the first kings may have been called Pul, and if so, certainly was the contemporary of Menahem of Israel, who, according to our chronology, ruled from 760 to 750. We may now safely assert that the difficulties which lie in the way of the synchronism which the Bible and the Assyrian inscriptions demand, as regards Menahem, Pul and Tiglat Pilesar, can be solved by the assumption that after the contemporaneous reign of Pul and of Menahem, Tiglat Pilesar in 738, his eighth year, received the tribute from the king of Israel, which had been imposed on Menahem by Pul, as the Bible asserts it. The statement that in the year 738 Tiglat Pilesar received 'the tribute of Minihimmi Samirinaai' does not refer to the personal presence of the latter. As the Assyrian campaign against Arpad took place in 754, in the fourth year before Menahem's death, perhaps the paying of tribute was then imposed on Menahem, and he was recognised by Assyria in that year.

This much is absolutely certain, that the king of Israel who ruled between 760 and 750 according to the Bible, was the contemporary of Pul according to the Bible, and that three years before the now fixed accession of Menahem, that is, in 763, a new dynasty, the second Assyrian dynasty, came to the throne. The first king, or one of the first, may have been called Pul or by a similar name, and may have been succeeded by Tiglat Pilesar II., who is clearly distinguished in the Bible record from Pul. Were it not for this distinction, the name Pul might be regarded as derived from that of Tuklat-Habal-Asar.[1] As it is implied by the inscriptions, in which Tiglat Pilesar makes no mention of his parentage, contrary to custom, it may be asserted that he was not of royal descent. If we connect this probable fact with the disturbance in the capital Assur, eighteen years before the accession of Tiglat Pilesar, it seems reasonable to infer that in that year 763 Pul was either deposed as the last king of the first Assyrian dynasty, or raised by force as a king unconnected with the first Assyrian dynasty.

---

[1] Compare Schrader, *Die Keilinschriften*, who identifies both.

We may now go farther, and assert that the synchronism of Menahem and Pul, required by the Bible, according to our chronology excludes the otherwise possible hypothesis, that Pul was the last king of the first Assyrian dynasty. This assertion is confirmed by the tradition transmitted by Alexander Polyhistor, the friend of Sulla (born 138 B.C.), who had access to the writings of Berosus. For according to this tradition the list of the kings of the first Assyrian dynasty led to Belêus (Pul), who is thus shown to have been the first king of the second Assyrian dynasty, which we have proved came to the throne in 763, therefore eighteen years before Tiglat Pilesar. As this possible Pul is said to have been succeeded by an upstart sovereign, raised by force, and who fixed the succession in his own family until the destruction of Nineveh, we may connect the name of this king, Belêtaras, with the second part of that of Tiglat Pilesar, or Tuklat-Habalasar, probably a leading general, who succeeded Pul in 745.[1]

The synchronism assumed to be required by Assyrian inscriptions between Tiglat Pilesar and Azariah, or Uzziah of Judah, though impossible as late as the year 742, to which the inscriptions have been referred, becomes possible by our chronology up to 748, or three years previous to Tiglat Pilesar's accession. But we do not assume that the latter was Pul's co-regent and commander of the army. Uzziah's reign of fifty-two years ended in 748, so that he was a contemporary of Menahem of Israel. According to the Bible, both Uzziah and Menahem are contemporaries of a 'king of Assyria' called Pul; yet according to the inscriptions, on which the name of Pul has not yet been found, these two kings of Judah and Israel are supposed to have been contemporaries of Tiglat Pilesar. We hope to show, that this interpretation of the inscriptions is erroneous with regard to the supposed synchro-

---

[1] Polyhist. Eus. Chron. Can. I. 4.

nism between the reigns of Tiglat Pilesar and Azariah-Uzziah, and that the inscriptions do not necessitate the assumption that these kings were contemporaries. What we have proved with regard to Menahem can be as firmly established with regard to Azariah.

The inscription now generally assigned to Tiglat Pilesar IV. states that this king annexed to Assyria several districts of Hamath with their cities, which 'in faithless rebellion' had gone over to 'Azariah (Uzziah) of Judah.' Why should this rebellion not have taken place in the time before the accession of Tiglat Pilesar? If so, it may have taken place in the reign of Pul, and the inscriptions of Tiglat Pilesar would only confirm the Biblical statement, that Uzziah, as well as Menahem, were contemporaries of Pul, not of Tiglat Pilesar. This they are, according to our Hebrew chronology. Without disregarding the inscriptions, and without any forced interpretation of the Bible, both may be said to harmonise.

According to the inscriptions, Tiglat Pilesar received tribute from a king of Judah called Yahuchazi Jahudai. This name clearly refers to Ahaz of Judah (739–725), who was for twelve years the contemporary of Tiglat Pilesar (745–727). During the Syrian campaign (734–732) 'against Damascus and the Philistines,' Tiglat Pilesar may be assumed to have succoured Ahaz of Judah, who was attacked by Pekah of Israel (748–728), by Rezin of Damascus, as well as by the Philistines and Edomites. Ahaz joined the Assyrian ally at Damascus, which city was captured by Tiglat Pilesar after a long resistance. According to the inscriptions, Rezin had fled into a certain city, probably to Damascus, where he may have met with his death, to which the Bible refers.[1]

Pekah of Israel (748–728), the Pechacha of inscriptions, ruled seventeen years contemporaneously with Tiglat

[1] 2 Kings xvi. 5–9. Compare for this and the following the *Chronology of Sennacherib* by G. Smith, to whose assistance and suggestions, as also to Mr Sayce, Dr. Birch, and Mr. Basil Cooper, the author is deeply indebted.

Pilesar. Pekah's successor, Hosea (728–720), the Husie of inscriptions, whom the Assyrian claims to have set up, but probably confirmed, came to the throne one year before Tiglat Pilesar's death, and was contemporary of Shalmaneser IV. (727–722) for five years. According to Biblical account, the city of Samaria would seem to have been captured by Shalmaneser, who besieged it, but according to Assyrian accounts, this occurred between the two possible years 722–720, and therefore during the reign of Sargon (722–705). The inscriptions refer to Sargon as to 'the punisher of the broad Beth-Omri,' and 'the destroyer of the city of Samaria and of the entire Beth-Omri.' Sargon himself refers in an inscription to his siege and capture of the city. The ninth year of Hosea, in which the king of Assyria took Samaria,[1] is according to our chronology the year 720. It follows, that it was Sargon who made Hosea a prisoner.

Hezekiah (725–697), the Hazakiahu of inscriptions, was the contemporary of Sargon during the seventeen years of the latter's reign, and he ruled eight years contemporaneously with Sennacherib (705–680). We now come to the most important test for the correctness of our chronology. According to the Bible, the Assyrians first entered Judah ' in the fourteenth year of Hezekiah.'[2] This year synchronises with the eleventh of Sargon, 711 B.C., when he made an expedition to Ashdod.[3] We may therefore assume that Sargon, the then 'king of Assyria,' was with the army, but that his son and successor Sennacherib, with whom the future important events were directly connected, as leader of the Assyrian vanguard, entered the territory of Judah before Sargon, and was for this reason (or for others) connected in the text with this first Assyrian expedition against Judah,

---
[1] 2 Kings xvii. 6.
[2] 2 Kings xviii. 13; Is. xxxvi. 1.
[3] For the sixfold, if not sevenfold, synchronism referring to the year 711 B.C., see p. 50.

SARGON BEFORE JERUSALEM. 43

when, as shown by a new interpretation of the tenth and other chapters of Isaiah, Sargon seems to have besieged Jerusalem and there imposed the tribute on Hezekiah, which Sennacherib enforced ten years later.[1]

According to the inscriptions, Sargon ruled at least three years in Babylon as the Arkaianos of the Ptolemæan Canon, who reigned five years, after having deposed in the year 709 Mardok Empados (Emlados or Emplados?), the Marudachus-Baldanes, or Merodach (Berodach) Baladan of the Bible, who ruled twelve years according to the Babylonian annals. The embassy of Merodach to Hezekiah, referred to in the book of Isaiah, took place in the year 711, just before Sargon's campaign to Ashdod and Judah. The king's illness, accompanied by the promise of a further reign of fifteen years, took place so many years before the death of Hezekiah in 697, that is in 712–711, the fourteenth of his reign, and was followed in that same year by the 'coming up' of the Assyrians, in the reign of Sargon, his son Sennacherib possibly leading the vanguard.

It is clear that the object of Merodach's embassy was an alliance between Babylon, Judah, and Egypt, and that the pretended enquiry after 'the wonder which was done in the land,'[2] cannot have had any reference to the solar eclipse of 689, which took place eight years after the death of Hezekiah, to whom the embassy was sent. More probable is the hypothesis, that the astronomical wonder, recorded to have resulted in a relative retrogression of the sun-dial, was connected with an alteration in the inclination of the dial or column. The sun-dial of Ahaz may have been introduced as an Assyrian innovation whilst this king was the vassal of Tiglat Pilesar, and even introduced an altar from Damascus, as probably also the astronomical symbolism of the Assyrians. This possible Assyrian sun-dial may have been replaced by another,

[1] See the important Essay of Mr. Sayce, *Theol. Rev.*, Jan. 1873.
[2] 2 Chron. xxxii. 31; comp. Is. xx. 5, 6.

perhaps by a Babylonian sun-dial, which marked a comparative retrogression of ten degrees, as it might also be taken to mark symbolically the intended receding from an Assyrian to a Babylonian alliance.

In the year 701 the campaign of Sennacherib against Hezekiah took place, which according to the Assyrian account led to a victory. The contemporary advance of Tirhakah, king of Ethiopia (Cush), possibly accompanied by pestilence, had no doubt something to do with the retreat of the Assyrians.[1] The Assyrian inscriptions refer to Manasseh as the contemporary of Asarhaddon, which synchronism offers no difficulty, as the former reigned from 680–668, and the latter from 697–641. Thus all required synchronisms are proved, which the Bible and the inscriptions require.

ASSYRIAN AND HEBREW SYNCHRONISMS.

Assyria	Judah	Israel	Contemporary Years
Shalmaneser II. 850–823		Ahab 857–854 Battle of Karkar and of Ramoth Gilead, 854 Jehu 847–810	5 years 24 years
Pul (?) 763–745	Azariah (Uzziah) till 748	Menahem 761–750	Pul with Azariah 3, with Menahem 10–11 years
Tiglat Pilesar IV. 745–727	Ahaz 739–725	Pekah 748–728	Tiglat Pilesar with Ahaz 12, with Pekah 17 years
Shalmaneser IV. 727–722		Hosea 728–720	Shalmaneser with Hosea 5 years Sargon with Hosea 2 years
Sargon 722–705	Hezekiah 725–697		Sargon with Hezekiah 17 years
Sennacherib 705–680			Sennacherib with Hezekiah 8 years
Asarhaddon 680–668	Manasseh 697–641		Asarhaddon with Manasseh 12 yrs.

[1] 2 Kings xix. 9.

RESTORATION OF THE BABYLONIAN DYNASTIES AFTER BEROSUS.

We now give a table of the Babylonian dynasties according to Berosus, and as restored by us.

THE DYNASTIES OF BEROSUS RESTORED.

No.	Dynasty	Kings	Length of Reign	Years B.C.
I.	Chaldæans	86	34,080	unhistorical as regards 34,080
II.	Medes	8	224	2458–2234
III.	Unknown (Urukh) . .	11	[242]	2234–1992
IV.	Chaldæans (Kudur Mabuk).	49	458	1992–1534
V.	Arabians (Hammurabi) .	9	245	1534–1289
VI.	Assyrians	45	526	1289–763
VII.	Assyrians	8	[138]	[763]–625
VIII.	Chaldæans	6	87	625–538
IX.	Persians	10	207	538–332 (331)
			1003	

It will be seen, that assuming the second Assyrian dynasty to have come to the throne in 763, which we hope to have proved, the length of reigns assigned by Berosus to the first Assyrian and the Arabian dynasties fixes the dates 1289 and 1534 as the respective accessions of the same, leaving exactly 700 years between the accession of the Arabian and of the first historical Chaldæan dynasty, the date of which is fixed by Berosus. As Hammurabi reckoned 700 years from his accession to Urukh, it is now proved that this most ancient chronological date of the cuneiform inscriptions known to us is historically correct. The years of the respective accessions of the two Chaldæan dynasties, 2234 and 1992, are leading dates in the Hebrew chronology, the former being implied as the year of Shem's birth, the latter as the exodus from Haran, now proved to be contemporary with the accession of the first king of the second Chaldæan dynasty, probably Kudurlagamer of Elam.

It is, therefore, no longer necessary to assume, that in the first year of the era of Nabonassar, 747, at the commencement of the astronomical canon, the second Assyrian dynasty in Babylon came to the throne. But although we have changed this supposed date for 763, and starting from that have altered the hitherto received dates for the accessions of the three preceding dynasties, the length of reigns which we know from Berosus has been accepted, and only the rule of the second historical dynasty, hitherto not known, has been fixed at 242 years, thus giving a total of 1903 years from the accession of the second historical dynasty commencing with Urukh to Darius Codomannus, or from 2234 to 331.

Thus the statement of Callisthenes is confirmed according to which the astronomical calculations of the Chaldæans reached to 1903 years before Alexander. Callisthenes accompanied Alexander the Great to Asia, and communicated this statement from Babylon to Aristotle, his relative and teacher, whilst the philosopher Simplicius, who has transmitted this information in his treatise 'de Cœlo,' fled to Chosroës, king of the Persians, in the beginning of the sixth century A.C. The correctness of this statement, corroborated by Pliny, has lately been assailed.[1]

ORIGIN OF BABYLONIAN AND OF ASSYRIAN POWER.

We have seen that Medes ruled in Babylon from 2458 until the accession of the first of the post-Median eleven kings, of Urukh, in 2234. These Medes, the Madai of the Bible, we have proposed to identify with the Hyksos who seem to have entered Egypt soon after 2234, and also with the 'Arabians' who twenty-four years after the expulsion of the Hyksos ruled in Babylon from 1534. We distinguished from these Medes the Assyrians, who may

[1] Pliny H. N., vii. 57; T. H. Martin, *Annales de Ph. Chr.* xiv. 254; confirmed by Oppert, *Hist. des Empires*, etc. p. 7.

be referred to in Genesis under the name of Ashur, who went forth out of Shinar 'and builded Nineveh' with other cities, according to a possible reading of the text.

The account given about the first establishment of Nimrod in the plain, which probably the Assyrians (Sumir) first called Shinar, connects Nimrod with the city of Erech, to which the name of Urukh may refer. But the name of Nimrod carries us much farther back, to the period which preceded the capture of Nimrod's Babylon by the Medes of Berosus in 2458 B.C. Powerful reasons have lately been given [1] for connecting, if not identifying, the name Nimrod with the divinity Merodach, showing that in the Bible Nimrod stands in the same relation to Asshur as in the inscriptions Merodach is placed with regard to Ashur. Nimrod is in Genesis called 'the son of Cush.' There was a Cushite population in Elam probably already in the pre-historic times of Nimrod, whether or not these Cossaei of classical writers may be ethnically connected with the East, from whence came the first inhabitants of Shinar referred to in the Bible. We hold 'the land of Cush,' adjoining the Eden of Genesis and watered by the Gihon, to be the lowland of the Jichoon, Amu or Oxus. Over Non-Aryans or Cushites (Turyans?), originally come from the countries about the Hindu-Cush, Nimrod 'the son of Cush' may have ruled. Those who on a monument of Ramesses II. are designated as of 'the heretic race of Kesh' were Cushites from the Gihon—Euphrates, whose ancestors lived on the Gihon—Oxus, after which also the Nile was called Gihon.

Not Nimrod, but Urukh (Orchamus, Urchamus), whose rule began in 2234 B.C., was the builder of the temple, tower, or house of Bel. The Biblical account about the Tower of Babel, connected as it is with the confusion of tongues, may be connected with Urukh's tower of 'the seven lights of the earth' at Borsippa, then the planets, but previously the Pleiades, as we shall prove in another

[1] Rev. A. Sayce, paper read at Biblical A. S., April 1873.

place.¹ After the long rule of the Medes and on Urukh's accession in Babylon, the Non-Babylonians (Iranians?) whom the Babylonians (Indians?) subjected, or who willingly remained in Babylonia, would naturally not understand the commands of their foreign rulers.

We have no reason whatever to doubt the historical accuracy of the Chaldæan historian Berosus, that in 2458 Babylon existed, and was captured by the strangers whom he calls Medes. A Chaldæan could no more have invented such a foreign rule than the Egyptians could have invented the sway of the Hyksos. Every doubt on the correctness of this fact, and of the date 2458, vanishes before the positive proof that, like Berosus, the Hebrews begin their history with that date, with which, for one reason or another, they unquestionably connect the birth of Shem. Babylon was therefore in the possession of the Iranian Medes from 2458 to 2234, when Urukh established his rule there. Five years later these Medes as Hyksos seem to have ruled over a part of Egypt as the 12th dynasty, upon which the 15th followed, and of which monuments have been found in the Hyksos fortress Avaris. For if to the 511 years of the Hyksos rule over the whole of Egypt, which ended with their final expulsion in 1558, B.C., we add the 160 years which Africanus gives to the 12th dynasty, we get 2229 B.C. for its accession.

We have seen, that according to alleged Manethonian tradition, the commencement of the Hyksos rule, soon after 2234 according to our chronology, synchronised with the growth of Assyrian power, so that Nineveh may have been built any time after 2234. This assumption is in the first place confirmed by the assertion of Sargon II. in an inscription of his, that 350 Assyrian kings had preceded him. Considering the marvellous exactness of the 700 years of Hammurabi, and the 600 years of Sennacherib's inscription, we have no longer

¹ *The Pleiades and the Zodiac.* The name Borsippa (Babylon) has been explained to mean 'confusion of tongues.' Compare Lenormant, *Fragments cosmogéniques de Bérose.* 1872.

any ground for discrediting this statement. The 350 ancestors of Sargon would require even a longer period than from 2234 to 722. That the Assyrian Royal power was established so early is confirmed by the dates of Ctesias, born at Cnidus in Caria, contemporary of Xenophon. Ctesias was companion of Artaxerxes Mnemon, and lived seventeen years at the Persian Court, leaving Persia in 398. Of course he could not have written his history of Persia in twenty-three books without knowing the cuneiform inscriptions, the chronological accuracy of which is now so firmly established, and he may have known the traditions of the priests. According to Ctesias, from the foundation of Nineveh until Pul, Assyrian kings ruled for more than 1200 years. From 763, these 1200 years and more would reach beyond 1963. We saw that like Tanis also Nineveh may have already existed in the year 1992 when Abraham left Haran, and when Chedorlaomer began his reign. The Assyrians not being mentioned on either side may be explained by the assumption that they acknowledged the authority of the King of Elam. This supposed state of things would be changed by the repulse of the Elamite Lord of the West.

On the whole, it is perhaps not improbable that Ashur went forth from Shinar to build Nineveh with its temple of Ishtar, soon after 2234, when Urukh established himself at Babylon, after that the Medes had ruled there for 224 years, whose first king, according to Iranian tradition, was called Zoroaster.

EGYPTIAN CHRONOLOGY.

If we have succeeded in proving that, according to Hebrew Chronology the fifth year of Rehoboam's reign falls in the year 928 B.C., this year, in which Jerusalem is recorded to have been captured by Shishak, must synchronise with the twentieth or twenty-first of Sheshenk I. For, according to the Silsilis inscription, stone was cut in that quarry of Upper Egypt in the twenty-first year of Sheshenk I. for the temple of Thebes. As we here find a record of his conquest of Judah, it is generally inferred that this campaign took place in the twenty-first or in the twentieth year of that Pharaoh's reign. It will be a satisfactory test of the correctness of our Hebrew Chronology, if the year 948–947 B.C., as the year of Shishak's accession —that is, the twenty-first or twentieth before his capture of Jerusalem—can be shown to harmonize not only with our fifth year of Rehoboam's reign, but with the most probable of the transmitted Manethonian dates, and to lead to other synchronisms between the history of Egypt and of other countries.

It follows from our Hebrew Chronology, that if Shishak was on the throne at Bubastis in 948-947, or twenty to twenty-one years before the fifth year of Rehoboam's reign, Shishak was the contemporary of Solomon during the end of this king's reign, in perfect harmony with the recorded flight of Jeroboam from Jerusalem to the court of Shishak, where the former remained till he heard of Solomon's death. A Manethonian statement which has never been drawn in question, confirms our date for Shishak and thus the synchronism hitherto despaired of between this Pharaoh and Solomon. Manetho, Egyptian priest of the city of Sebennytus, who lived during the reign of Ptolemy I. (305-285 B.C.), states positively that the first Olympiad was celebrated in Egypt during the forty years' reign of Petubastes, the first king of the twenty-third dynasty. Between the accession of Petubastes and that of Shishak, first king of the twenty-second dynasty, Manetho is reported by Africanus to have reckoned 116 or 120 years. It is generally admitted that, according to the monuments, more time must be allowed for the entire reign of the twenty-second dynasty. But even were we to reckon 120 years from our date for the first year of Shishak's sole reign, 935, the year of the first Olympiad in 776 B.C., would have fallen in the reign of Petubastes. It will be seen that the first Olympiad fell in his twenty-fifth year.

We shall now try to show that the year 711 B.C. fell within the reign of the last king of the twenty-third dynasty, that is, of Zeth, long recognised as the Sethos whom Herodotus helps us to connect with the advance of Tirhaka of Ethiopia.[1] In that very year (711 B.C., being the fourteenth of Hezekiah), according to a tradition transmitted by Jerome,[2] Tirhaka slew Sevek or Sabako, and according to an inscription of Sargon, the Ethiopians then sued for peace.[3] The Egyptian tradition communicated to Herodotus, out of jealousy to the Ethiopians, abstained from mentioning Tirhaka or Sabako. But if, as the tradition implies, Tirhaka marched his army from Ethiopia during the reign of Zeth-Sethos, and if in 711 Tirhaka slew Sevek I. or Sabako, then Zeth-Sethos of the twenty-third, and Sevek I. of the twenty-fifth dynasty must have been co-regents. According to Egyptian tradition Tirhaka advanced contemporaneously with Sennacherib's campaign in 701, not with Sargon's in 711. But the story related by Herodotus clearly implies that it was the first advance of Tirhaka's vast army into Egypt, during which Sethos was abandoned by the army. The mistake of connecting Zeth-Sethos (742–711) with Sennacherib (705-680) and not with Sargon (722-705), arose from the fact that Tirhaka was the contemporary as of Zeth-Sethos and Sargon, so of Sennacherib, of Asarhaddon and Assurbanipal. Because Sethos was assumed to have been the contemporary of Sennacherib, the army of the latter was supposed to have been destroyed by a night-miracle, just as that army is by the Hebrews recorded to have been destroyed ten years after the death of Sethos. Thus Sethos was also connected with the myth

---

[1] Bunsen's *Egypt*, II. 504; IV. 507.
[2] Cod. Tuk. of Jerome's Chron. ad ann. 1306 = B.C. 711, cited by Unger, and pointed out to me by Mr. Basil Cooper.
[3] Compare Botta, 65, 1; 83, 13, 84; 155, 1-12.

about the mice gnawing the bow-strings and shield-thongs of the Assyrians.[1]

This may be considered sufficient circumstantial evidence to prove that Sethos must be connected with Tirhaka's first advance into Egypt in 711, when Tirhaka asked Sargon for peace and slew Sevek I. As it is certain that the name Sethos cannot refer to Sevek-Sabaco, it may now be asserted that Sethos is the Zeth of the twenty-third dynasty, and that the year 711 falls within his reign; but as the end of it cannot be determined, it is doubtful in what year of Petubastes the first Olympiad was celebrated. If Zeth died in 711, the first of Petubastes would have been eighty-nine years earlier, or 801 to 800 B.C., the first Olympiad falling in his twenty-fifth year. We cannot go higher, but the year 776 may have corresponded with a later regnal year of Petubastes. We shall now give reasons for assuming that Zeth died in 711 B.C., and that Petubastes came to the throne in 800.

Africanus, or Julius the African, priest or bishop of Emmaus-Nicopolis in Judæa at the beginning of the third century, the most trustworthy recorder of Manethonian chronology, gives 116 (120) for the duration of the twenty-second dynasty. As Manetho referred to the year 776 B.C. having fallen within the reign of Petubastes, we may assume that his 116 years referred only to so many regnal years for the twenty-second dynasty as reached to the first of Petubastes. It can therefore be hardly considered as a chance-coincidence, that according to our chronology 114 years elapsed from the death of Shishak to the first of Petubastes, or from 914-800 B.C. We may now go further and suggest, that as Eusebius and Africanus absolutely agree in assigning 130 years to the duration of the twenty-first dynasty, the 114 which Africanus according to a

[1] The people of Troas are said to have revered mice 'because they gnawed the bow-strings of their enemies' (Eust. II. 1, 39), and Apollo Smintheus was represented on coins of Alexandria-Troas with a mouse in his hand (Müller, anc. art. 361, 5, cited by Wilkinson in Rawlinson's Herodotus II. 141.)

variant assigns to the same dynasty, in truth may have marked the duration of the following or Shishak-dynasty. For Shishak's reign was not reckoned in consecutive chronology, for reasons to which we shall presently refer. Certainly the accession of Petubastes was not supposed to mark the end of the twenty-second dynasty, and it is probable that the later kings of the same, as also those of the twenty-fourth, and Sevek I., that is, all the co-regents of Petubastes and his successors from 800 to 711, were regarded as of secondary importance. Of Zeth-Sethos we know that he had a fleet in the Mediterranean.

We have thus shown, that from the latest possible year for the accession of Petubastes, 800 B.C., to our date for Shishak's death there are 114 years, that is, only two years less than the 116 which Africanus assigns to the twenty-second dynasty, even if we do not assume that the 114 years which just precede the 116 in the list have been transposed from the twenty-second to the twenty-first dynasty. For this hypothesis we have given the plausible reason, that 130 years are assigned to the twenty-first dynasty as well by Africanus as by Eusebius, so that Africanus cannot have assigned 116 years to the same. These facts and arguments tend to show that the accession of Petubastes took place in 801-800 B.C., and that Zeth-Sethos accordingly died eighty-nine years later, or 711 B.C., that is, in the same year when Tirhaka killed Sevek I.

We now proceed to show why we place the last year of Shishak's reign in 914. Syncellus, Vice-Patriarch of Constantinople, about 800, has recorded 34 years for the reign of Shishak I., probably referring to the total of his regnal years, whilst the twenty-one years recorded by Africanus and Eusebius refer to his sole reign. Dating the 34 years from 948, our year for Shishak's accession, he died in 913, and his sole reign, on the above hypothesis, commenced in 935, that is, in the year before Solomon's death. In the year 914 Osorkon I. came to the throne, Psusennes of the twenty-first dynasty being yet alive. Mr. Cooper seems to us to have proved that the thirty-sixth year of Psusennes is contemporaneous with the first of Osorkon, the former not being described as dead in the inscription on the Nilegod statue, which mentions both. Accordingly Psusennes would have survived Shishak I. by about a twelvemonth. Lepsius has already pointed out the family relations between the twenty-first and the twenty-second dynasties. According to Mr. Cooper's scheme the marriage between Shishak's son Osorkon I. and the daughter of Psusennes II., led to a political treaty between the rival dynasties, according to which Shishak I., from the date of that political marriage, became King of entire Egypt.[1] According to our chronology this marriage and the commencement of Shishak's sole reign took place in 935, as shown above. Because Psusennes survived him, Shishak's reign was not reckoned in consecutive chronology.

The twenty-second dynasty, founded by Shishak, was not superseded by the twenty-third dynasty of Petubastes. It continued to reign contemporaneously with the latter, according to Mr. Cooper's Chronology, till 753, the first year of Bokhoris I., of the twenty-fourth dynasty, as we shall soon show. The year when the reign of the twenty-second dynasty came to an end may be differently computed, inasmuch as the starting-point for such calculation may either be the accession of Shishak as co-regent, or the commencement of his sole reign, or the year of his death. Accepting our date for Shishak's accession as determined by Hebrew Chronology, he came to the throne at Bubastis in 948, or 148 years before the accession of Petubastes in 800 B.C., whilst 114 years elapsed from Shishak's last (914) to the first of Petubastes. From our year for the death of Shishak to Mr. Cooper's first year for Bokhoris I., or from 914–753 are 161 years. On the monuments a minimum of 140 years is recorded. Allowing for the fifteen years assigned in the lists to Osorkon I., this number would be raised to 154.

[1] App. note V.

ACCESSION OF RAMESSES II. 55

Thus the accession of Shishak in 948 B.C., fixed by our fifth of Rehoboam (928), with which the monumental twenty-first (twentieth) of Shishak synchronises, is confirmed by the 161 years from the last year of the twenty-second dynasty (753 B.C.) to the last of Shishak (914 B.C.), whose reign was not reckoned for stated reasons. Again, our dates for Shishak are confirmed by the fact that the last twenty-one years of his reign, or of his sole regency, commence in the year before Solomon's death according to our Hebrew Chronology. The flight of Jeroboam to the court of Shishak, and this Pharaoh's capture of Jerusalem a few years later, imply that Shishak was in possession of undisputed power in Egypt during the last year of Solomon's reign. Finally, we repeat it, the 114 years from the first of Petubastes to the last of Shishak, or from 800–914, may account for the 114 years which Manetho seems to have assigned to the twenty-second and not to the twenty-first dynasty.

The 130 years assigned to the reign of the twenty-first dynasty by Africanus and Eusebius may be dated either from Shishak's accession (948), or from the commencement of his sole regency (935), or from the year of his death (914). It seems most probable that they were reckoned from the first year of his sole and undisputed sovereignty, 935, and, if so, the first of the royal high priests of Tanis, Smendes, came to the throne in 1065, or three years after the accession to the judgeship of Samuel, the introducer of prophet schools in Israel. This synchronism is not without significance, seeing that the prophetic party went with Jeroboam to Egypt.

Dating the 135 years of Africanus from 1065, the twentieth dynasty came to the throne with Ramesses III. in 1200 B.C. For the reign of the nineteenth dynasty Eusebius gives 162 or 194, and Africanus 204 or 209 years. We accept the 162 years of Eusebius, according to which the nineteenth dynasty came to the throne with Ramesses I. in 1362. Sethos I. reigned according to the monuments at least 17 years. We thus get 1344 for the accession of Ramesses II., and twenty-two years for the reign of Horus and his successors, the accession of the former being in 1384, as fixed by the year of the accession of Tuthmoses III., which may now be regarded as certain.

According to Orosius, the Pharaoh of the Exodus died in 1558. Accepting this tradition, the Pharaoh of the Exodus must have been Amenophis I., whose reign of thirteen years seems to have marked the second Hyksos rule of thirteen years according to Manetho. The Egyptian historian's Pharaoh of the Exodus, as we have seen, was an Amenophis and the successor of a Tuthmoses, Amoses, or Ahmes. The date 1558 for the death of Amenophis I. is confirmed by our Hebrew date for the Exodus, 1563, which falls within the thirteen years of the reign of Amenophis I., whose reign from 1571–1558 is finally confirmed by the fact, that accepting the acknowledged regnal years for his two successors Tuthmoses I. and II., we get 1515 for the first of Tuthmoses III., whose accession in that year is confirmed astronomically. Starting from 1200 B.C., as the first regnal year of Ramesses III., the 393 years of Manetho, according to Josephus, between the end of the 19th dynasty and the expulsion of the Hyksos, reach to 1593 B.C., and to the 22nd of Ahmes, who, according to Manetho, reigned 25 years after this event. During the last three years Amenophis may have been co-regent. This seems to be confirmed by the fact, that no later regnal year of Ahmes than his 22nd is mentioned. According to the inscription of Admiral Ahmes the capitulation of Avaris took place in the 6th year of Ahmes. We place his accession in 1598 B.C.

Perhaps the most satisfactory confirmation of the synchronisms thus far established between Manethonian and monumental dates of Egyptian history on the one side, and Israelitic, Assyrian, and Babylonian dates on the other, may be derived from the coincidence, to which we have already referred in passing, that whenever, according to our Egyptian Chronology, an Egyptian Pharaoh advanced through Syria to invade Mesopotamia, the

THE PHARAOHS AND THE PHILISTINES. 57

Philistines, Purusata or Pulusata, cognate with the Sharutana (Sardinians?) and other known or probable allies of the Egyptians, ruled over the Israelites, according to our Hebrew Chronology, as the following table shows:—

Foreign Rulers in Israel.	Contemporary Reigns of Pharaohs.
1518–1510 Chusan Risathaim	Tuthmoses II. 1537–1515. Tuthmoses III. 1515–1461.
1470–1452 Moabites	Amenophis II. 1461–1452.
1372–1352 Philistines	Horus and others 1384–1362. Ramesses I. 1362–1361. Sethos I. 1361–1344.
1312–1305 Midianites	Ramesses II. 1344–1278.
1217–1109 Philistines and Ammonites	Ramesses III. 1200–1168.
1108–1148 Philistines	First successors of Ramesses III.

Beginning with the last synchronisms, we find that the twenty years of the last Philistine rule correspond with the twenty years following on the year of the death of Ramesses III., fixed as the length of his reign is by the thirty-two years of the Great Harris-Papyrus. Again, we find that thirty-one years of the previous Philistine rule fell within the reign of Ramesses III., of whom the monuments state that he was the ally of the Sharutana, which people had also assisted Ramesses II. during his Asiatic expeditions. The maritime portion of these Sharutana assisted the Tsakruri and other enemies of the Pharaoh; and from the fact that the land of the Sharutana extended to the Mediterranean, as did the land of the Philistines, the ethnic relation of the Sharutana and the Philistines gains in importance.[1] It would be absolutely certain that Ramesses III. followed the sea-coast, if Maka-Tyra which he attacked were certainly Tyre and not Migdol. The statement that the sea supplied Tyra with fish, though in favour of the rock-island, is not conclusive. This road by the sea-coast must have been preferred to that to the east of the Dead Sea, as facilitating the supply of the advancing army with food, and the protection from maritime attacks. The Pharaohs, therefore, could not have advanced through the sea-bordered land of the Philistines without ensuring their alliance, as well as that of the cognate Sharutana. The object of this alliance must have been to protect the line of communication between Mesopotamia and Egypt. Now, as the Israelites had no dealings with the Egyptians after the Exodus and before the time of Solomon, their records never mentioning them in that time, it is impossible to assume that they were the allies of the Egyptians. On the contrary, they were dangerous foes, and likely to interrupt the Egyptian lines of communication unless prevented by force from doing so. The rule of the Philistines and other nations of Palestine over the Israelites was a necessity for the Egyptians.

We submit, that a Chronology according to which the chief foreign dominions over the Israelites were contemporaneous with the reigns of those Pharaohs who advanced to Mesopotamia, or attacked Palestine for other reasons, has thus much in its favour. It may be regarded as an important coincidence, that our first year of Sethos I. (1361), in which, according to the monuments, he overran Syria, falls within our fourth-last Biblical period of the Philistine rule over the Israelites, from 1372–1352. The rule of the Midianites, from 1312–1305, falling within the reign of Ramesses II., may be explained in like manner, as that of the Moabites can be connected with the exploits of Amenophis II., and the reign of Chusan Risathaim with the Asiatic campaign of Tuthmoses III. and the policy of his predecessor.

By historical synchronisms, by monumental evidence, and by probably Manethonian traditions, we hope to have proved that Shishak-Sheshenk I. came to the throne in 948 B.C.

Starting from this year, and after having fixed the accession of Amenophis I. and of Tuthmoses III., we have tried approximatively to fix the regnal years from Shishak to Amos. Again, starting from 948 B.C., we shall now try to fix the regnal years from Shishak to Amasis, by the aid of a suggestion of Mr. Cooper about the twenty-third dynasty. Before we give Mr. Cooper's scheme for the reign of the twenty-fourth, or Bokhoris dynasty, it is important to recapitulate the sixfold synchronism which we have established with reference to the year 711 B.C., and which synchronism has suggested some of the preceding Egyptian dates.

The year 711 B.C. is shown to have been:
1. The fourteenth of Hezekiah.
2. The year of Hezekiah's illness and recovery.
3. The year of Merodach Baladan's embassy.
4. The year of the first campaign of the Assyrians under Sargon to Ashdod and Judah, when Sargon, 'the subduer of the land of Judah,' seems, according to Isaiah x., to have besieged Yavani of Ashdod's ally Hezekiah at Jerusalem and to have made him tributary.[1]
5. The year when Tirhaka slew Sevek I. (719–711), whom Sargon, after the battle of Raphia in 720, could still distinguish as Sultani from the Pharaoh.
6. The year when the 'King of Meroe' asked Sargon for peace, to whom Sevek had given up Yavani of Ashdod, the ally of Hezekiah.
7. The year 711 was probably the last of the reign of Zeth-Sethos, the contemporary of Sevek I., like whom he may have been slain by Tirhaka, inasmuch as the dynasty of Petubastes and Zeth-Sethos probably reigned from 800-711.

To this sixfold, and probably sevenfold, synchronism may be added a possible eighth; for, according to Diodorus, Herodotus placed in 711 the revolt of the Medes under Dejoces, whom Diodorus calls Cyaxares.[2]

If the twenty-fifth dynasty of Ethiopians certainly ascended the throne of the Pharaohs in 719, the twenty-fourth or Bokhoris-dynasty, following upon the twenty-second dynasty of Shishak, must have ruled longer than is usually assumed, seeing that hardly more than from 154–161 consecutive years can be given to the reigns of

[1] Mr. Sayce in *Theological Review*, January 1873.
[2] Diod. II. 32. About the Daiuccu of cuneiform inscriptions, transported in 715 to Hamath, and the probable confusion in the Greek accounts about Deiokes and Astyages of the mythical Azi-dahâka with an historical Dai-uccu, see Sayce in App. Note VI. comp. Rawlinson's *Herodotus*, III. 446.

the twenty-second dynasty, without reckoning the reign of Sheshenk I. Mr. Cooper has proved, that reckoning backward from the first year of Pharaoh Sevek I. (719) the twenty-fourth dynasty came to the throne, as Josephus states after Manetho, in 753, having ruled thirty-four years, according to variants in Eusebius and Syncellus, and that there were three kings of this dynasty. Bokhoris I. reigned from 753-747, Tefnacht (including Piankhi) from 747-725, Bokhoris II. from 725-720 (719), the six years of this king, whom Sevek I. burned alive, having been put down in the list of Africanus as the total of regnal years for this dynasty.

The dates for the twenty-fifth and twenty-sixth dynasties offer no difficulty and are firmly established. The Ethiopian dynasty reigned fifty-four years, from 719-666, and the twenty-sixth or second Saite dynasty 139 years, from 666-527. This is confirmed by the twenty-seven years and a half of the Apis-inscription, between the accession of Taharuka and his successor Psammetikh, as also by the epigraphic forty years between the accession of Neku (Necho) and Amosis (Amasis), the commencement of whose reign in 572-571 seems to have coincided with Nebuchadnezzar's real or expected conquest of Egypt to which the book of Ezekiel refers.

TABLE OF EGYPTIAN DYNASTIES.

Dynasty

XVIII. followed by stranger kings, 236 years, 1508-1362 B.C.
  XIX. 162 years, 1362-1200.
  XX. 135 years, 1200-1065.
  XXI. 130 years, 1065-935.   XXII. 34 years for Sheshenk I., 948-914.
                                         " 21 years for his sole reign, 935-914.
                                         " 114 years from death of Sheshenk
                                            to accession of Petubastes, 914-800.
  XXII. (*contd.*) 101 years from XXIII. 89 years, Petubastes 800-760.
      Sheshenk's death to   "   Osorkon 760-752.
      accession of Bokhoris   "   Psammus 752-742.
      I., 914-753.   "   Zeth (Sethos) 742-711.
  XXIV. 34 years, 753-710.   "
  XXV. 54 years, 719-666.
      Sevek I., 710-711.   "   Death of Zeth, 711.
  XXVI. 139 years, 666-527.

EZRA AND THE PURIM, 515–510.

As already pointed out, the consecration of the second temple took place in 516, the seventieth year after the destruction of the first temple in 586. With these seventy years the prophecy of Jeremiah was connected. We have shown how the historical events of these seventy years led to the theory of the Messianic Millennium. We proceed to point out, that the time of fifty-eight years which has hitherto been assumed to have elapsed between the events narrated in the sixth and the seventh chapters of the book of Ezra must be reduced to one year—that consecutive events are recorded in consecutive chapters. The narrative has been obscured by the titles given to rulers in Babylon. The consecration of the temple under Scrubbabel is described as having taken place in the sixth year of Darius, and the mission of Ezra in the seventh year of Artaxerxes.

The title 'Darius,' from Darayawush, Tariyawaus of the inscriptions, is connected with ' dhâri ' or ' firmly holding,' and thus is connected with the idea of rule. Darius means the ruler or king. Xerxes, from khshaya-arsha, means venerable king. Artaxerxes, Artakhshatra, is by Herodotus translated as a compound of ' Arta ' great, and ' khshatra ' warrior or king, but may be connected with the Arya or the Arii, whom Herodotus calls Artaioi, and which is the name of the ancestors of the Persians. Artaxerxes means 'king of the Aryans.' It follows that both 'Darius' and 'Artaxerxes' were originally understood as titles, not as proper names, just as 'Pharaoh' was understood in Egypt. Both titles might be given to one and the same person. We may assume that the account of the consecration of the temple was written by a different scribe than the following chapter on Ezra's mission. A very probable assumption would make Ezra himself the narrator of the latter event. Thus the two titles 'Darius' and 'Artaxerxes' may have been given to the Darius or king Hystaspes-Vashtaspa, the 'Artaxerxes' or 'the king of the Aryans.'

No other ruler than Hystaspes had such claims for receiving the ancient Aryan title Artaxerxes. For he was the real founder of the Persian monarchy, and his possessions extended from the Indus to the Nile. Thus we have also suggested that the king of the book of Esther was Hystaspes, here called Ahasuerus, Achashverosh, Achashures, 'strong king,' a compound word having the same meaning as Artakshatra, and from which Khsha and Shah is derived.[1] The king of the book of Esther is described as 'Ahasuerus' (the king) 'which reigned from India even unto Ethiopia.' Also the division into provinces may be connected with the Satrapies, into which Hystaspes divided his empire, according to Herodotus and the book of Daniel. To Vashtaspa likewise refers the name of Esther's predecessor, Vashti, as Vash-ti, the wife of Vash, formed like Baal-ti. Esther or Hadassah is thus clearly the same name as Atossa, the queen-mother of Xerxes in the 'Persians' of Æschylus.[2]

If Hystaspes could be called Darius, 'ruler,' and also Artaxerxes, 'king of the Aryans,' that is of the Persians, then Ezra's mission to Jerusalem took place in the year after the consecration of the temple, in the seventh year of Hystaspes, 515, and not, as hitherto assumed, in the seventh year of Artaxerxes Longimanus in 458. Hystaspes was the king and Esther the queen, when Ezra, and after him Nehemiah, were appointed as governors. The last year of Nehemiah's rule coincides with the battle of Marathon.

[1] Sir Henry Rawlinson, in Rawlinson's *Herodotus*. Steph. Byz. *Artaea*. Lassen und Benfey's *Keilinschriften*. Fürst, Chald. Dict. III. 444–455.

[2] About Virgil's Elissa, the Dido of the Phœnicians, about the possible connection between the seven conspirators and the 'Seven Chiefs of the Persians and Medes,' in the book of Esther, and about the meaning of Vistâspa, 'Possessor of the Horse,' as the possible origin of the legend about the horse of Darius, see *Keys of St. Peter*, 225 f. On the book of Judith as a possible allegory referring to the ays of Purim, see *Einheit der Religionen*, i. 664 f.

The principal events from 536 to 510 are the following:

First Caravan, 536.—Cyrus, the first 'Artaxerxes,' or king of the Aryans, permits the return. Foundations of the temple and of the walls laid about 534, under Serubbabel and Joshua. Nehemiah present, but not Ezra.

Second Caravan, 520-516.—Darius Hystaspes, the second Artaxerxes, or king of the Aryans, renews the edict of Cyrus. With the help of the Samaritans the temple is finished and consecrated. Public reading of the law by Ezra. Great synagogue under Ezra. Covenant sealed with Nehemiah. Peace and concord established.

Ezra and the Purim, 515-510.—In 515 Ezra is sent as governor, with power over life and death. Serubbabel is not mentioned by Ezra. The seven visions of Zechariah refer respectively to the seven years from the second to the ninth year of Hystaspes, from 520-513. The first vision, about the return of God's grace, refers to the renewal of the edict of Cyrus by Hystaspes in 520. The second vision, about the measuring of the temple, refers to the recommencing of the building of the same, with the help of the Samaritans, in 519. The fifth vision refers to the year 515 and to the roll containing the curse, and to the removal of the ephah to the land of Shinar to build a house unto the wickedness. It is evident that this vision, coinciding with the year of Ezra's short mission, must refer to the principal event of Ezra's governorship, to the expulsion of all Jews who had allied themselves with strangers, especially with the Samaritans. As we know from Josephus that many dissatisfied Jews, including members of high priestly families, asked the Persian king to permit them to build a temple in Samaria like that in Judæa, and that they built the temple at Gerizim, the date of the building of the same may be approximatively fixed at soon after 515.

We should expect that the comparatively few Jews

belonging to the two tribes of Judah and Benjamin would be easily overcome by the remnants of the ten tribes in Samaria, and that the despotic measure of Ezra would lead to bloody conflicts. An hitherto overlooked passage in the 'Antiquities' of Josephus may be referred to the year of Ezra's governorship.[1] Bagoses, general of the army of Artaxerxes (Hystaspes), was a friend of a certain Joshua, brother of the high priest Johannan at Jerusalem, and he had promised his friend to procure him the high priesthood. Because of this promise of the Persian general in Samaria, a quarrel arose between the two brothers whilst they were in the temple. Joshua irritated the high priest, whereupon the latter killed his brother in the temple. In consequence of this, Bagoses entered Jerusalem, forced his way into the temple, and punished the Jews for the murder of Joshua during seven years. It does not follow that Bagoses remained seven years in Jerusalem; but in order to enforce tribute and obedience, he probably left a sufficient army in Judæa, which was not withdrawn till the seven years were over, that is, about fourteen months after the events which led to the Purim memorial.

The book of Nehemiah commences with a statement which has hitherto not been at all explained, and which directly confirms our suggestion, that the passage just cited from Josephus must be placed at the end of Ezra's governorship, and previous to that of Nehemiah. 'In the twentieth year' of Artaxerxes (Hystaspes), that is 502, Hanani, one of Nehemiah's brethren, came, with certain 'men of Judah,' and informed the royal cup-bearer that the remnant which were left of the captivity in the province were 'in great affliction and reproach,' that the wall of Jerusalem was 'broken down, and the gates thereof burned with fire.' This is what we should expect if, owing to the expulsion of the strangers by Ezra, two camps had been formed among the Israelites in Judæa, a

[1] *Ant.* xi. 7.

Judæan camp and a Samaritan camp, and if Bagoses, the Persian commander in Samaria during the rule of Haman at Babylon, had taken Jerusalem by force, and punished the Jews for seven years because of the fratricide committed in the temple by a high priest.

Although Josephus refers, a few pages earlier, to a Cyrus whom the Greeks called ' Artaxerxes,' it did not occur to him that the Artaxerxes of this account, which he faithfully transmits, may have referred to Hystaspes. Assuming the Artaxerxes to be Longimanus, Josephus explains that before this time Eliashib had died, who may be presumed to have gone to Jerusalem, either in 536 or 520. We suggest that it was the entry of Bagoses into Jerusalem in 515, which put an end to Ezra's governorship, if not to his life, in the tenth month of that year. The influence of ' the stranger ' in Israel became increased by the contemporary rule of Haman, the enemy of the Jews. This would lead the agagite, or royal vicar, to make use of the presence of Bagoses in Jerusalem to crush the party of the separatists, to which Ezra seems to have belonged. To upset Haman in Babylon must therefore have appeared as the sole means of saving the separatist party. The beauty of Esther, the Benjamite, was to bring this about, and did bring it about.[1]

We may now assert that the first feast of Purim, preceded by the setting up of Mordechai in the place of Haman, took place on the fourteenth and fifteenth Adar (Nisan) of the twelfth year of Ahasuerus, that is, of Darius Hystaspes, in 510, or 2383 years ago! Eight years after Mordechai's accession, Nehemiah was sent as governor to Jerusalem, and it was in 502 that the walls were consecrated, and the second solemn reading of the law took place. It is uncertain how long Nehemiah remained in Jerusalem, but he continued as governor for twelve years. The last date of an historical

[1] *Ant.* xi. 0, 1; about the murder of Joshua and Zechariah, App. Note VII.

event recorded in the Old Testament is that of his last journey to Jerusalem in the thirty-second year of the king, that is, in 490, when, after the loss of the battle of Marathon, Hystaspes had lost his influence in Europe, and probably in Syria.

YEAR OF THE BIRTH AND YEAR OF THE DEATH OF JESUS.

According to Josephus, Herod died five days after the execution of his son Antipater, and there is no valid reason to doubt that Herod's death took place either at the beginning of B.C. 4, or at the end of that year, January 18th, 3 B.C.[1] An attempt has been made by a conscientious chronologist[2] to show, that the first year of Herod, counted from the death of Antigonus, should be reckoned from B.C. 36, 126 years being deducted from Nisan B.C. 162, in the spring of which year Judas Maccabæus is considered to have set up the Asmonæan throne. In confirmation of this calculation reference is made to Clement of Alexandria, who places the birth of Jesus in 'the 28th year'*(of the Egyptian era of the battle of Actium, 2nd September B.C. 31,) thus in B.C. 3-2, when first the census was ordered to be taken in the reign of Augustus.[3] Clement connects this statement directly with the assertion, that Jesus suffered in the 16th year of Tiberius, that is, that he was crucified in the year after his baptism, and that from the time he suffered to the destruction of Jerusalem were 42 years and 3 months. Accordingly the crucifixion would have taken place in the year 29-28 A.D., which is impossible. We have no reason to trust Clement's information about the birth of Jesus more than that about his death.

[1] For the latter view, see the able essay by Quandt: 'Chronologisch-geographische Beiträge.' 1872.
[2] Bosanquet, in *Transactions of Society of Biblical Archæology,* i. 93-105.
[3] Strom. i. 21.

THE DEATH OF HEROD.

Clement's statement about the time 'when first the census was ordered to be taken in the reign of Augustus,' that is from B.C. 3-2, seems to be equally incorrect. It is difficult to support it by the statement in St. Luke's Gospel that 'the taxing was first made when Cyrenius (Quirinus) was governor of Syria.' It would be necessary to assume that the order had been given B.C. 4-2, soon after the possible appointment of Quirinus to his first governorship, late in the year A.D. 4, according to Professor Zumpt's discovery, and that the taxing was concluded, or that another census took place, during his second governorship, beginning in the year B.C. 6.

It must be allowed, that on this supposition, the decree which went out from Cæsar Augustus that 'all the world should be taxed' might be interpreted to have referred to the entire Roman Empire, and distinguished from the taxing of the inhabitants of Judæa, which could not have taken place till after this country was annexed as a province to the Roman Empire in the year A.D. 6, when, after the banishment of Archelaus, as Josephus correctly states, Quirinus was certainly appointed as governor, whether for the first or for the second time.

Again, on the supposition that several years elapsed between the decree of the general census and the taxing in Judæa, it might be explained, why no mention is made anywhere of the census in the year A.D. 6, which was of a local character. But it would remain unexplained, why in the tablet of Ancyra the assumed general census of B.C. 3-2 is not noted, although three enumerations of Roman citizens in the reign of Augustus are therein mentioned, that is, in B.C. 27, B.C. 7, and A.D. 14. In the latter year Augustus had the epitome of his public acts drawn up on bronze tablets at Rome, which epitome is mentioned by Suetonius, and of which the citizens of Ancyra, in Galatia, had a copy made, cut in marble blocks, and placed in the then capital of the Roman province of

Galatia, in a temple dedicated to Augustus and Rome, in the ruins of which the tablet of Ancyra was found.

We have no reason to doubt that a census in Judæa took place when Quirinus was governor and after the annexation of this province to the Roman Empire, A.D. 6, or later. It is possible that the Gospel after St. Luke refers to two events, which happened at distinct periods: to the Imperial decree that all the world should be taxed, and to the later taxing of Judæa. If so, the former would refer to the general census in B.C. 7, and the latter to the provincial census A.D. 6.

In this year a census took place by order of Quirinus, according to Josephus, and he adds, that on this occasion Judas of Gamala, the Gaulonite, whom he also calls a Galilean, attempted a revolt of the people, asserting 'that this taxation was no better than an introduction to slavery.' St. Luke himself, in the Acts, seems at first sight to refer to the taxing in the year A.D. 6, inasmuch as he connects it with the rising of 'Judas of Galilee.'[1] Josephus distinguishes from Judas of Gamala another Galilean, Judas of Sephôris, who raised a revolt at the time of Herod's death, but whom Josephus does not connect with a taxing. The Acts seem to refer to this Judas of Sephôris, the chief city of Galilee, by the reference to his having drawn away many people after him, who perished or were dispersed. This account agrees best with the recorded fact, that in consequence of the revolt at the time of Herod's death, Sephôris was wasted by Varus, A.D. 3. In both passages St. Luke might be supposed to refer to one and the same time, that is, to that of Herod's death, if a taxing in Judæa at the time of Judas of Sephôris could be proved by other evidence than by the above passage in the Acts, and if Josephus, as well as coins from that time, did not show that Varus, not Quirinus, was then governor. Josephus mentions him as present when Antipater was brought to judgment, a few days before Herod's death. An over-

[1] Jos. *Ant.* xviii. 1, 1; comp. xx. 5, 2; Acts v. 37.

ingenious attempt has been lately made to get over even this difficulty, by the assumption that Quirinus, though not governor at that time, may have then held a distinguished military position in Syria. This is indeed shown to have been possible by a reference to an inscription, from which it appears that under the (military?) rule of Quirinus a census was taken in the Syrian city of Apamea, and war was made against the Ituræans, about the time when, according to a possible interpretation of the Acts, a taxing took place in Judæa, that is, at the time of Herod's death. We are asked to assume that, though the taxing could not have commenced under the governorship of Quirinus, it may have ended during his possible first rule, not many months after Herod's death.[1] Of course this is possible.

What more immediately concerns us, is the record in the Gospel after St. Luke, where the journey of Joseph and Mary from Galilee to Bethlehem is stated to have been caused by the decreed taxing, and to have led to their being taxed. According to the positive gospel-statements, they were enrolled at Bethlehem, and the child was born at the time, when Quirinus was governor in Syria, whilst these events took place before the death of Herod. It is quite certain that the possible first governorship of Quirinus cannot have commenced before the end of B.C. 4, but it is perhaps not equally certain that Herod died shortly before Easter in B.C. 4.

It has been lately argued by a most careful chronologist,[2] that Herod's death, which occurred after a lunar eclipse and before a Passover, may have taken place after the eclipse of March 13 B.C. 4, and yet on the 18th January of the year 3 B.C., reckoning the first Nisan as the 18th of March, in accordance with the festive calendar of the Jews. Thus more time would be allowed for the events recorded by Josephus as having taken place between the eclipse and the death of Herod, as also between the death and the Passover. On the usual reckoning the first Nisan

[1] Quandt, l.c. 21-25.   [2] Ibid. l.c. 4-12.

fell on the 29th of March, and the day of the Passover on the 11th of April. Plausible reasons are given for the assumption that a longer period than 18 days are required between the eclipse and the death, and more than 11 days between the death and the Passover. But this hypothesis is irreconcileable with the fact, now established, that the Mishna-rule was often followed by the Israelites, and that accordingly the first year of a king might not have lasted more than one day. Josephus certainly reckons the days from the 29th of March to the 11th of April as a full year. Herod died B.C. 4.

For this date is not only implied by the statement of Josephus, but it is also confirmed by his reference to a lunar eclipse in the night of the day when, an indefinite but probably short time before his death, several persons were burnt to death. Such an eclipse took place 28 days before the Passover, on the 13th of March, B.C. 4.[1] At the Passover of that year Archelaus, having succeeded Herod, slew 3000 Jews and Samaritans opposed to his government. As Herod died early in B.C. 4, and as Quirinus could not possibly be appointed governor before the end of that year, Jesus cannot have been born before the death of Herod and yet after the appointment of Quirinus as governor of Syria. The governorship of Quirinus cannot possibly be connected with the time of the birth of Jesus of Nazareth.

We attribute no weight whatsoever to the connection of the birth of Jesus with a taxing, as we hope to prove that he was born about fourteen years before the Christian era, and that the commencement of the same in the fourth year after Herod's death was connected with this historically impossible time, not by chance, but with the design of connecting the destruction of Jerusalem in

[1] Another and a total eclipse of the moon occurred twenty-eight days before the Passover, on the 10th of January B.C. 1. Mr. Bosanquet holds that Herod died between that day and the Passover following, of the year B.C. 1, and thus arrives at the autumn of B.C. 3 or the spring of B.C. 2 for the birth of Jesus, 'as laid down by St. Luke.'

the year A.D. 70 with the symbolism of the mysterious number seventy.

We have shown, that designed alterations can be detected in the Hebrew text of the Old Testament, the final revision of which did not take place till after the return from Babylon. The text of the New Testament was not finally revised before the time of Constantine. It has been proved by the most ancient Syrian version which we possess, that 'The Gospel of the Hebrews' accounted for 17 generations from Abraham to David. Yet in our Gospel according to St. Matthew, and moreover in that part which alone can be proved to have been directly translated from the Hebrew, the genealogy of Jesus Christ is divided into three parts, and it is especially mentioned, that each of these divisions conntais twice seven or fourteen generations. Thus the 17 generations from Abraham to David are reduced to 14, and the 13 generations from Salathiel to Jesus are increased to fourteen. This was done apparently with a view to point out the sanctity of the number seven,[1] and perhaps also in order to suggest that the 13th genealogy refers to Jesus, the 14th to his second coming as Messiah. Since the two designed alterations of the Hebrew text which we have pointed out are directly or indirectly connected with the mystic number seventy, the above alteration in the Greek text of the New Testament, connected as this alteration is with the mystic number seven, must be regarded likewise as made with a design to serve dogmatic purposes. We shall now substantiate our suggestion, that the nativity of Jesus, for a similar dogmatic reason, was placed in the year 754 of Rome, or in the year one of the Dionysian era, that is four years after the death of Herod, in spite of the unanimous statement in the gospels that Jesus was born during the reign of Herod.

---

[1] About the early and aboriginal connection of the holiness of the number seven with the seven stars of the Pleiades, see our work, preparing for publication, on *The Pleiades and the Zodiac.*

The commencement of the Christian era is incorrect, as first fixed by Victorinus or Victorius of Aquitania in 465, who dated it from the death of Jesus, and then by Dionysius Exiguus, a Scythian by birth, living as a priest in Rome from 530–536, who began the era with the birth of Jesus. It may be that the Dionysian era was fixed in accordance with a design of making the destruction of Jerusalem by Titus coincide with the mystic year 70, dated from the supposed nativity of Jesus.

The date of the birth of Jesus, to which attention can be shown to have been directed early in the second, if not in the first century, cannot be even approximatively determined by the statement in the Gospel after St. Luke, that Jesus was about thirty years old when he began to teach. This broad statement, originally perhaps a mere explanatory note or gloss, later received into the text, may be explained to refer to the age which public teachers must have reached, or surpassed, before being acknowledged as such.[1] But apart from this argument there is no reason for assuming that this statement must be connected directly with the preceding record about the baptism of John, in the fifteenth year of Tiberius, in 'all the country about Jordan.' Some time, probably from one to two years, must have elapsed between the fifteenth year of Tiberius, when 'the word of God came unto John,' and the time 'when all the people were baptized,' and when Jesus came to him to be baptized.[2] We are expressly told that it was not until Jesus heard that

[1] Compare Num. iv. 2; 1 Chron. xxiii. 3.

[2] According to Volkmar's exhaustive investigation John was put into prison from 30 to 31 B.C. He seems to us to establish the following points. John was imprisoned and put to death in the fortress of Machærus, which belonged to Aretas, when his daughter fled to her father before Herodias. After this separation of the daughter of Aretas, or after the marriage of Antipas with Herodias, Antipas cannot have disposed of Machærus. John was put aside as a demagogue, as Josephus states: and this was done before the separation of Antipas from the daughter of Aretas, and when he was on good terms and allied with the owner of Machærus. Volkmar, *Die Evangelien*, 22, 354, 658–660.

John had been cast into prison, that he began to preach in Galilee. It corresponds well with these facts and arguments, that, according to Justin Martyr, Jesus was 'thirty years old or more' when John began to preach, that is, before Jesus did so.[1]

We shall now try to prove conclusively that this statement in the Gospel after St. Luke cannot possibly have been originally connected with the fifteenth year of Tiberius so as to show Jesus to have been in that year, or a few years later, about thirty years old. We think it can be established by sound arguments that Jesus in that year 29 was at least forty-three years old.

As Herod died four years before our era, Jesus must have been born at least one year earlier. The recorded murder of the children at Bethlehem, connected with the birth of Jesus, need not refer to the last year of Herod. How many years before Herod's death Jesus was born cannot therefore be determined from the Gospel records. Justin Martyr's statement, that Jesus was born about 150 years before the composition of the first Apology, probably before 138, is too general to deserve notice. But the first Father of the Church who refers to the age of Jesus states that he lived between forty and fifty years.[2] Irenæus refers to a double authority, which is all the more remarkable, as it cannot be proved that before or in his time this was a debated question. He refers to 'the Gospel' and to the tradition of the elders who had lived 'with John' in Asia: 'From the fortieth to the fiftieth year a man begins to decline towards old age, which our Lord possessed while he still fulfilled the office of a teacher, even as the gospel and all the elders testify; those who were conversant in Asia with John, the disciple of the Lord, (affirming) that John conveyed to them that information.'[3]

---

[1] *Dial.* 88, 315.
[2] *Haer.* ii. 22. 4-6.
[3] Compare *Antenicene Christian Library*.

This statement is preceded by a reference to the thirty years. 'How could he have taught unless he reached the age of a master? For when he came to be baptized he had not yet completed his thirtieth year, but was beginning to be about thirty years of age.' It is added, that according to 'these men,' the first three Evangelists, 'he preached only one year, reckoning from his baptism.' It must be admitted that this looks like a later interpolation. For if Jesus had not yet completed his thirtieth year in or possibly after the fifteenth year of Tiberius, and yet lived from forty to fifty years, his crucifixion could not have taken place during the reign of Tiberius, which is a fact, as the Annals of Tacitus refer to it.[1] This fact must have been well known to Irenæus. The fifteenth year of Tiberius is the year 29, and Tiberius died certainly not later than 37 A.D., or eight years later. If Jesus was not more than twenty-nine years old in A.D. 29, he was not more than thirty-seven years old at the death of Tiberius.

It is thus proved, that Irenæus cannot possibly have connected his statement about Jesus having been between forty and fifty years old, with that in the Gospel after St. Luke about Jesus having been about thirty, or even not yet thirty as it is explained, when he came to be baptized, which was not before, but possibly after the fifteenth year of Tiberius, the year 29. The two passages absolutely exclude each other.

Yet Irenæus refers to 'the Gospel,' as well as to unanimous Apostolic tradition, when he asserts that Jesus was between forty and fifty years old when he died. We may therefore regard the passage in the third Gospel as a mere gloss which referred, as the passage in the works of Irenæus directly confirms, to the required age of a teacher, which was thirty years or more. Moreover this gloss was not intended to be connected with the time about the fifteenth year of Tiberius, and to show how old Jesus was on

[1] *Ann.* xv. 44.

or about that year. Whether this passage be so regarded or not, this much is certain, that Irenæus did not refer to the Gospel after St. Luke when he wrote, that his assertion about the age of Jesus was made on the double authority of ' the Gospel,' and the tradition of disciples of the Apostle John.

To what passage in any of the four Gospels, which Irenæus is the first to cite by name, can this learned Father of the Church have referred? What passage in the Gospels is there, besides the passage cited, which refers to the age of Jesus, and to which the testimony of ' all the elders who were conversant with John in Asia ' testified, affirming that the Apostle St. John ' conveyed them that information'? It must be a passage which, without the aid of an explanation of the initiated, would not have necessarily ' conveyed that information.' We shall now try to prove, that the passage in question is in the Gospel according to St. John, which, rightly understood, and as the Gospel explains, referred to the person of Jesus, ' to the Temple of his body.'[1]

The first question which arises is, whether those of the Jews to whom the words of Jesus were addressed could possibly have misunderstood their meaning, so as to refer them to the building of the Temple. We lay no stress on the probability that, in harmony with Eastern custom, Jesus pointed to his person with his hand when he spoke the words in question : ' Destroy this Temple, and in three days I will raise it up.' Also our argument does not require the very probable assumption, that among the people who surrounded Jesus, asking for a ' sign,' thus demanding an authority for his acts, were men in authority, that is, scribes, priests, and men belonging to the Temple-guard. On either of these allowable assumptions Jesus would have been understood as he wished to be understood. But the reference to the 'three days' must have prevented a connection of his words with the stone-

[1] John ii. 18-21.

Temple by those who knew about the resurrection, whether they, like the Pharisees, accepted that doctrine, or whether they refused to acknowledge it, like the Sadducees. The high-priests and Pharisees appearing before Pilate did connect the saying of Jesus about the three days with the resurrection. Again, not by true but by 'false witnesses,' whose testimony moreover did not agree, it was asserted, that Jesus had said within their hearing: 'I will destroy this Temple that is made with hands, and within three days I will build another made without hands.'[1]

The Jews, probably Sadducees, thus rightly referring the words of Jesus to his person, and following Jesus in the allegorical form of speech chosen by him, proceeded to refute him on his own ground, by expressing a doubt that Jesus could himself restore in three days what was the growth of forty-six years. 'Forty and six years was this Temple in building, and wilt thou rear it up in three days?' The following words commencing with 'but,' must therefore be taken in the sense of, 'now, he spoke of the temple of his body.'

It follows from this, that in the first year of his ministry Jesus was forty-six years old, just as the Gospel-statement implies, to which Irenæus refers as to the written authority for Jesus having lived between forty and fifty years. This assertion may now be connected with the passage thus explained. According to the same Gospel three years later, in the last year of the life of Jesus, the Jews said: 'Thou art not yet fifty years old, and wilt thou have seen Abraham?' Thus the connection of the former passage in the fourth Gospel by Irenæus with the tradition of those who had known the Apostle St. John becomes highly significant, and furnishes a new proof as to the connection of this Gospel with the beloved disciple and with the first three Gospels.[2]

---

[1] Mark xiv. 58; comp. Matt. xxvii. 62, 63.
[2] Verbal tradition is shown to have been the cause of Biblical development in the Old and the New Testament, in *The Hidden Wisdom of Christ*.

According to the so explained passages in the fourth Gospel, Jesus was forty-six years old in the first year of his teaching, and not yet fifty years old in the year of his death, in essential harmony with the statement of Irenæus. This Gospel refers either to three or (possibly?) to two years of his ministry. We regard the three years' ministry as conclusively proved.[1] Accordingly Jesus was in his forty-ninth year when he died.

The crucifixion of Jesus took place, as we have seen, during the reign of Tiberius, who according to Josephus reigned twenty-two years, five months, and three days.[2] It is doubtful whether this time is reckoned from the death of Augustus, or from the time that Tiberius was co-regent. But it is generally assumed that Tiberius was murdered in the beginning of the year 37, probably in March. Accordingly the year 36 is the latest possible for the death of Jesus. Now, the year 33 can be proved from the Gospels to have been the earliest possible year for the crucifixion, if we accept the forty-eight years of the Fourth Gospel and of Irenæus. Once more, as in the case of the false witnesses, a statement in another of the Gospels confirms the Fourth Gospel. According to the Gospel after Matthew, Jesus was twelve years old when, after the death of Herod, and after a stay in Galilee, he went with his parents to Jerusalem. Jesus cannot have returned from Egypt and gone to Jerusalem at the time of Easter in the year of Herod's death. He went there certainly not earlier than the year after it, or 3 B.C. It follows that in the year of Herod's death, 4 B.C., Jesus cannot

---

[1] See S. Sharpe, *The Chronology of the Bible*, 1868, p. 69–71.

[2] A confirmation of the statement in the *Annals* of Tacitus lies in the reported fact that Tiberius was dead when Pontius Pilate arrived at Rome, sent there by Vitellius, governor of Syria, in order to defend himself against the accusations of the Samaritans, who were being prosecuted like the Christians during the reign of Agrippa I., and who had risen under Simon (Magus?), about 35, thus possibly in connection with the crucifixion of Jesus, who had probably more followers in Samaria than in Judæa, and was by the Jews called 'a Samaritan.'

have been more than eleven years old, so that he cannot have been born before the year 15 B.C., and that after a life of forty-eight years the earliest year of his death was 33 B.C., the 19th of Herod, when, according to Cedrenus, Jesus died. In that year the Paschal full moon fell on Friday the 15th Nisan, so that the 14th Nisan lasted from Thursday to Friday evening, as in the year of the crucifixion according to the Gospels.

If Jesus was forty-eight years old at Easter in the year 33, it follows that he was born in 15 B.C.[1] Accordingly in the year of Herod's death, 4 B.C., Jesus was eleven years old, and the recorded murder of infants at Bethlehem of the age of two years and under refers to about the ninth year before Herod's death, 14–13 B.C. The journey of Joseph and Mary with Jesus when twelve years old to Jerusalem, probably with a view to the usual course of instruction in the law, took place in the year after the death of Herod, and less than two years after the return from Egypt, after a stay of about nine years in that country. In the fifteenth year of Tiberius, 29 A.D., Jesus was forty-four years old.

If Jesus, as a child, was nine to ten years in Egypt, he received his earliest religious instruction probably in Greek and in accordance with the text of the Septuagint. Thus the general reference of Jesus and his disciples to the Septuagint version would be explained, as also the unquestionable connection of the Gospel-doctrines with those of the Apocrypha or 'hidden writings,' which were in Palestine forbidden, but formed an important part of the Greek version of the Scriptures. Again, if the doctrinal enlargement and development of the Septuagint can be traced to a secret tradition of the initiated, made known in Alexandria to a large circle, but which continued to be a 'hidden wisdom' to the people in Palestine, the Jewish doctors at Jerusalem would naturally be astonished at a boy of twelve years old betraying an unusual knowledge, and later at a teacher who had 'never learnt' the Scriptures.

[1] On the 25th of December. See *The Pleiades and the Zodiac*.

DATE OF THE FIRST MARTYRDOMS. 79

YEAR OF THE MARTYRDOM OF ST. STEPHEN AND
ST. JAMES.

On the assumption that the death of the first martyr took place in the first year of the persecutor Herod Agrippa I., of Asmonean (Sadducean?) descent, that is in 41, the journey of St. Paul to Damascus and his conversion took place in that year, and as Agrippa's rule of terror lasted three years, a reason would thus be assigned for St. Paul's not returning to Jerusalem until three years after his conversion.

'About the same time,' or, as we explain, contemporaneously with the martyrdom of St. Stephen, summarily brought about by the persecutor, the Apostle St. James, brother of St. John, was beheaded by Agrippa, and St. Peter was put into prison, was marvellously led out of it, and he left Jerusalem for 'another place,' that is, for Rome, as we shall presently render probable. If St. Peter was put into prison in 41, it is certain that 'James, the brother of the Lord,' was in the same year, 41, set over the disciples at Jerusalem. For St. Peter refers to him and the brethren in the night of his marvellous delivery out of prison. During the three years of Agrippa's reign of terror, the Apostles seem to have been kept in more or less strict confinement, and probably for this reason, perhaps also because James was trusted by the Sadducees, the Apostles are in the Acts stated to have been exceptionally spared during the general persecution of Christians. The accession of the young Herod Agrippa II. in 44 seems to have put an end to these persecutions. To this time the following statement in the Acts may be referred. The Apostles were suddenly led out of prison by an angel, and they preached daily and openly 'the word of Christ Jesus.' Those who could three years earlier put to death St. Stephen and St. James, now were afraid of being stoned by the people when leading the Apostles out of the Temple.[1]

[1] Acts xii. 16; v. 12-42; viii. 1.

The possibility that the first two martyrs died in 41 will be raised to a probability, if it can be reasonably assumed, that during part of the three years which St. Paul spent in Arabia, that is, in the land east of Jordan, St. Peter founded the Roman Church.

ST. PETER AND PHILO IN ROME.

Seeing that the beheading of St. James 'pleased the Jews,' Agrippa proceeded to take St. Peter also, 'intending after Easter to bring him forth to the people.' By a marvellous interposition of Providence led out of prison on a certain night after Easter, just before Herod intended to bring him forth, he came to the house of Mary the mother of John Mark, 'where many were gathered together praying,' and Rhoda having announced the unexpected arrival, St. Peter beckoned with his hand unto the inmates of the house 'to hold their peace,' declared unto them how the Lord had brought him out of prison, and said: 'Go show these things unto James and to the brethren, and he departed and went into (unto) another place.' St. Peter had to flee for his life, and he must have tried to gain the sea-coast as quickly as possible. His nearest road would take him to Joppa, where he had quite lately made friendship with Simon the tanner. Thence he would perhaps go to Cæsarea, to his friend Cornelius, captain of the Italian band. From this place his further escape by sea or land would be easier. According to the Clementines, James was appointed after seven years 'from the passion of the Lord,' that is in 41, the first year of Agrippa I. Thus it is confirmed that St. James was in that year beheaded and St. Peter put into prison, whereupon he was delivered and went 'unto another place.' He met Simon at Cæsarea, and 'drove him away into Italy.' St. Peter followed him and had disputations with him at Rome.[1] In 42, St. Peter founded the Church at Rome according to the tradition transmitted and confirmed by Eusebius as well as by St. Jerome.[2] Both these learned Fathers of the Church attest, the one in direct connection with the first stay of St. Peter at Rome, that in this city St. Peter met with Philo of Alexandria. Eusebius adds, that this meeting led to 'familiar conversation' between the Apostle and the learned Alexandrian Jew, whilst the former ' proclaimed the Gospel to the inhabitants of that city.' The learned and impartial historian states that he regarded this as ' not at all improbable,' thereby implying, that this ' familiar conversation,' though not the meeting at Rome which led to it, was drawn in question by some in the fourth century.

In the Armenian version of the Chronicle of Eusebius, the second year of Claudius, or 42, is mentioned as the year of St. Peter's arrival in Rome, which year St. Jerome also mentions as the year of the foundation of the Roman Church. From this it follows that both Eusebius and St. Jerome had reasons to believe that Philo and St. Peter met at Rome in 42, that is, in the ninth year after the crucifixion of Jesus.

It must be regarded as the most remarkable of all recorded and clearly undesigned coincidences, that Philo fixes his one visit to Rome about the year 41, and that he leads us to assume that he remained there until 42. At the head of a deputation of Alexandrian Jews Philo appeared first before Caligula, and then his apology was read before the Roman senate during the reign of Claudius, which can hardly have been done when in January 41 the soldiers by force set up this emperor. In the first year of the Prætorian rule the senate can hardly have had time to consider the case brought forward by Alexandrian Jews. Everything

[1] Recog. i. 43; Constit. vi. 8; Hom. iii. 29 f.
[2] Eus. H. E. ii. 17. Compare 14 and Chron. (Armen.). Hier. Catal. i. 1.

tends to show that it was during Philo's prolonged stay for some indeterminable time after 41, that he met St. Peter at Rome. The undesigned coincidence between the time fixed for this meeting by Eusebius and St. Jerome, and the time fixed by Philo for his arrival at Rome, may be regarded as a remarkable confirmation of the Roman tradition in the Clementines, which moreover makes St. Peter travel from Jerusalem by Cæsarea to Rome in the very year 41 in which we place his departure from Jerusalem by Joppa and Cæsarea unto another place.

So long as St. Peter's absence from Jerusalem after his miraculous escape from prison cannot be connected with some other facts, or even with some other theory, the remarkable coincidence of dates permits us at least to assume that the tradition transmitted by the two most learned Fathers of the Church is correct, and that St. Peter did found the Church at Rome between the years 42 and 44, in which latter year we find him and St. Paul again at Jerusalem with James for fifteen days.

St. Peter and St. Paul jointly founded the Church at Antioch, probably between 44 and 45. At Corinth St. Paul met with Gaius, Aquila and Priscilla, the latter of whom had left Rome after the promulgation of the edict of Claudius (about 49–50?). The journey of St. Paul and Barnabas to Judæa, charged by the disciples of Antioch to convey the collections to relieve the Jews suffering by the famine, took place probably in the year of that famine, 45–46. The apostolic council took place from 54 to 55, if fourteen years after St. Paul's conversion in 41. His later journeys, including his stay of two years at Ephesus, may have taken place from 56–59, his last journey to Jerusalem at latest in 60, his departure from Cæsarea in the autumn of 65, his arrival at Rome in the spring of 66, and his martyrdom, perhaps contemporaneously with that of St. Peter, in 68 or 69, probably before the death of Nero in June 68. All dates after A.D. 44 are more or less uncertain.

RETROSPECT AND CONCLUSION.

A CONSECUTIVE chronology is the best proof of an uninterrupted historical tradition. We are in possession of a sequence of historical dates, preserved and transmitted by the Babylonians as well as by the Hebrews, and reaching to the year 2458 B.C. This year marks an era of Babylonian and the starting-point of Hebrew Chronology. The Babylonian tradition connects it with an historical event, the capture of Babylon by a foreign nation, whom the Chaldæan historian Berosus calls Medes. The Hebrew records connect that same year with what is there designated as the birth of Shem. For on this assumption all our synchronisms have been obtained. 'Two years after the Flood,' we are told, ' Shem was 100 years old;' from which it follows, accepting our date for the birth of Shem, that what in Genesis is termed the Noachian flood, took place in 2360 B.C.

The Hebrews, whose ancestors had lived in ' Ur of the Chaldees,' further connected with a Babylonian date the departure of Abraham from Haran, Naharayn or Mesopotamia. We have reasons to regard as the movements of a powerful tribe, what is related in Genesis as a family history, the journey of Abraham, with Sarai and Lot and the souls which they had gotten in Haran, from that country through Canaan into Egypt.

For, 367 years after the Noachian flood according to Genesis, that is, according to our Chronology, in 1992 B.C., when this migration took place, a new dynasty came to the throne at Babylon, according to the now firmly established dates for the Babylonian dynasties of Berosus. The cuneiform inscriptions speak of a Kudur-Mabuk, and, after the divinity Lagamer, a king of the same family might be called Kudur-Lagamer, who, like Kudur-Mabuk and Chedorlaomer, may have been 'King of Elam.' The first king of the Berosian dynasty which acceded to the throne in

Babylon in the year 1992, when Abraham left Haran, possibly called Kudur-Lagamer, was certainly a contemporary of Chedorlaomer, and probably identical with him. It being now proved that the migration of Abraham and his party from Mesopotamia was contemporaneous with the accession of a new and probably Elamite dynasty in Babylon, the movements of the Elamite Chedorlaomer may be connected with Abraham's movements. The probability gains ground, that his journey to Egypt, where the Hyksos were then ruling, was directly connected with political considerations, and that the Hyksos and their allies took part in the battle of Shiddim. We have, therefore, now no longer any reason to doubt that the Hebrew historian, Josephus, had good reasons to give credence to the statement of the Greek historian and friend of Herod and Augustus, Nicolaus of Damascus, that Abraham (having pursued Chedorlaomer to Damascus) conquered Damascus and ruled there shortly after his having left Haran.

Knowing the year of Chedorlaomer's accession, we also know that in his fourteenth year, or 1979 B.C., the battle in the valley of Shiddim took place. Between the exodus from Haran and the exodus from Egypt the Mosaic records mark a period of 480 years, of which 400 years were by the Hebrews passed in Egypt. The Mosaic Exodus is thus shown to have taken place in the year 1563 B.C. According to Orosius, the Pharaoh of the Exodus died five years later, in 1558 B.C. The year 1515 B.C. being astronomically fixed for the accession of Tuthmoses III., the duration of the reigns of his two predecessors, Tuthmoses II. and I., according to Manetho twenty-two and twenty-one years, carry us from 1515 to 1558, when according to Manetho, Amenophis I. died, who is thus shown to have been the Pharaoh of the Exodus. The Hebrew date for the Exodus falls within the thirteen years reign of Amenophis I., according to Manetho, whose tradition about a second rule of the Hyksos for thirteen years before their final expulsion is thus confirmed.

RETROSPECT AND CONCLUSION. 85

We are therefore entitled to record a threefold synchronism of the highest importance. The year 1563 B.C. is the Hebrew date for the exodus from Egypt. The year 1558 is the date when the Pharaoh of the Exodus died, according to the statement of the Spanish presbyter Orosius, the friend of St. Jerome, and who, during his long stay in Africa and Syria, seems to have drawn his information from trustworthy sources in the fifth century. Finally, between the year 1558 and the astronomically fixed year for the accession of Tuthmoses III. in 1515, lie the forty-three regnal years which Manetho places between the death of Amenophis I. and the accession of Tuthmoses III. Given the year 1515 B.C. for the accession of Tuthmoses III., the year 1558 is the Manethonian date for the last regnal year of Amenophis I., whilst the same year is given by Orosius for the death of the Pharaoh of the Exodus, which, according to the restored Hebrew Chronology, took place in the year 1563 B.C., or five years before the final expulsion of the Hyksos. Thus Hebrew tradition, Egyptian tradition, and later African or Syrian tradition, confirm each other.

The period from the Exodus to the building of the Temple is one of 592, not of 480 years. Josephus twice mentions 592 and twice 612 years for this period, thus making it end either with the foundation or with the dedication of the Temple. For the following reasons we insist that 592 must be adopted instead of 480, given in the first book of Kings.

1. St. Paul must have known, that from the division of the land until Samuel the Prophet were 450 years. If he was right, the period from the Exodus to the building of the Temple must have comprised a much longer number of years than 480. The forty years of Moses, from the Exodus to his death, suffice for the demand of a longer period. Accepting the 450 of St. Paul, and adding the forty years of Moses, and the five years of Joshua before the division of land on the one side, and

on the other three years of Solomon's reign, the forty of David and twenty-two of Saul, thirty-two years are left for Samuel, and we get 592 years. Thus the Scriptural dates, added to the 450 years of St. Paul, give exactly the 592 years which Josephus assigns to the period from the Exodus to the Temple. St. Paul and Josephus drew from one and the same historical tradition, by which they in this instance both corrected the Scriptures. It follows from this with mathematical precision, that the judgeship of Samuel, the duration of which is not given in Scripture, lasted thirty-two years; that all the periods given in the Book of Judges and in the first of Samuel as referring to this period, find their place in the enlarged frame of 592 years, and that the undetermined period from the death of Ehud to Barak's victory is limited by twenty years.

2. Jephtha assigned in round numbers 300 years to the period from the division of the land until the first year of his judgeship. This is only then approximatively correct, if we accept 592 instead of 480 years. According to our chronology this period was from 1518 to 1199 B.C., and included 319 years.

3. The synchronisms which result from our Hebrew and our Egyptian Chronology show, that the dominions of Moabites, Philistines, and Ammonites over Israelites were contemporaneous with the advances of Pharaohs through Canaan into Mesopotamia.

4. It is only by accepting the 592 years which the Hebrew records can be shown to require for the period from the Exodus to the building of the Temple, and by reckoning these 592 years from 1563 B.C., our date for the Exodus, that we have obtained without exception, and by accepting Hebrew dates, all the synchronisms required between the histories of the Hebrews, Assyrians, Babylonians, and Egyptians. Among these is a sixfold if not a sevenfold synchronism with regard to the year 711 B.C., which may be regarded as the most remarkable in ancient history.

RETROSPECT AND CONCLUSION.

Although as yet unable to produce a consecutive chronology of the Assyrians, the harmony now established by the known Assyrian dates between Hebrew Chronology and the Canon of Ptolemy, and with Egyptian dates, permits us to assert that the continuousness of the cuneiform annals is thereby confirmed, that no interval need be assumed in Assyrian history, nor any interregnums in that of Israel. All these nations possessed and carefully preserved historical chronological annals. It is owing to chronological dates preserved in cuneiform inscriptions that the regnal years of Babylonian dynasties can be determined from the year 2458 B.C., the Berosian date for the accession of the Medes, to the accession of Cyrus in 538, thus showing an uninterrupted chronology of 1920 years.

With regard to Egyptian Chronology, we submit that the most trustworthy Manethonian dates can be ascertained, that by a certain system of co-regencies they harmonise with the monumental dates, that they can occasionally be confirmed by astronomical calculations, and that they lead to remarkable synchronisms. The most important of these are contemporaneous events recorded by Egyptian and by Hebrew Chronology. The now established synchronism between Solomon and Shishak fixes the date for the capture of Jerusalem, and thus enables us, by accepting Manethonian dates, to assign to the Pharaohs of the eighteenth, nineteenth, and twentieth dynasties, who advanced through Canaan to Mesopotamia, such regnal years as correspond with the Hebrew dates for foreign dominions over the Israelites. At the time when these Pharaohs required the alliance of the Philistines and cognate nations in Canaan, the Philistines, Moabites, and Amorites can be shown to have ruled over the Israelites according to the Biblical records, from which synchronism we are led to surmise that the foreign rulers were the allies of the Egyptians.

It would seem that according to the scheme propounded in this Essay, possible if not approximatively correct dates can be assigned to the reigns of Manethonian dynasties, from the eighteenth to the twenty-sixth, extending over a consecutive period of eleven centuries, or from the approximate date for the accession of Ahmes to the death of Amosis or Amasis, from about 1600–527 B.C.

After this retrospect of the chief results of our chronology, we refer in conclusion to their indirect bearing on prehistoric times. The early existence of an hereditary tribal tradition of initiated, and the Eastern origin of this tradition,[1] first verbal, then written, is an increasingly probable hypothesis, by which the continuity of chronology and likewise the development traceable in holy writ can be best explained. The symbol, differently interpreted by the initiated and the uninitiated, formed the point of union between these two classes of human society, and thus between science and religion. As a rule, symbols were framed in perfect harmony with, and contained nothing contrary to tradition. A higher knowledge of what had been transmitted faithfully from generation to generation, would enable the initiated, not only to establish connecting links between a less enlightened past and a more enlightened present, between religion and science, but to mark the development of the future, prophetically though not chronologically.

Occasionally symbols or rules of faith were formed by stewards of tradition, not in harmony with history, and thus with the ever-developing Divine enlightenment, but with a view to real or supposed exigencies in the religious life of mankind. When new symbols ceased to take the place of ancient symbols, tradition became stagnant, symbols petrified, and barriers were erected between science and religion.

The existence of an esoteric knowledge or hidden wisdom is confirmed by the now established fact that St.

[1] Compare 'The Hidden Wisdom of Christ, or History of the Apocrypha.'

Paul and Josephus drew from one and the same non-written tradition, when they corrected an important date in holy writ. The existence of mysteries referring to the relations between the creature and the Creator, which were known to the few, unknown to the many, led to a publication of these truths in an allegorical form, well adapted to the immediate purpose, and sanctioned by those who regarded the secretion of mysteries as necessary for the preservation of class privileges. The preaching of the good news of ' the mysteries of the kingdom of heaven,' of the Gospel, to the poor and uninitiated, was a gradual one. At first by parables only, the seed of the Word of God, the doctrine of the Spirit of God, of Christ, in the hearts of men, was sown broadcast by ' the Son of Man' and 'the Son of the living God,' whilst the chosen few, according to the Gospel, St. Peter as the first among them, were instructed to proclaim from the housetops the more perfect Divine knowledge which had been whispered into their ears.

The hidden wisdom led to the use of the metaphorical, symbolical, allegorical, and parabolic forms. Whether and to what extent the initiated, or stewards of mysteries, interpreted figuratively the recorded miracles, cannot now be determined. The Biblical symbol of 7,000 years with its Millennium must be given up. The earliest period of Hebrew Chronology has been designedly shortened to 1656 years, being converted into twenty-three periods of seventy-two years, or Pleiades periods.[1] This designed alteration, as also that by which the 592 years were shortened into 480 years, has been made for dogmatic reasons, connected with the sanctity of the number seven, and this regardless of historical tradition. Likewise the date of the birth of Jesus of Nazareth has been designedly altered, and apparently for the similar dogmatic reason, of letting the destruction of Jerusalem coincide with the

[1] See our forthcoming works: 'The Pleiades and the Zodiac,' and 'The Symbol of the Cross among all Nations.'

seventieth year after the commencement of the Christian era.

All designed alterations of historical tradition now pointed out, if confirmed by the criticism which the sacredness of the cause demands, ought to be eradicated from the Bible. Of this collection of Scriptures the least that can be said is, that it is the book of undesigned coincidences. Holy writ is based on moral law, on conscience, and therefore contains a Divine revelation. In all ages the Father of the Spirits of all Flesh has spoken to man in manifold measures and fashions by His Spirit, His Word, His Christ. This Divine operation by which God 'in Christ' reconciles the creature to the Creator, this manifestation by which 'the day-spring from on high' was ready and willing to visit mankind at all times, was purposely hidden before the eyes of the people by spiritual leaders, who, to preserve their caste privileges, did not bring them up in the saving knowledge that every man's conscience is of Divine origin, ought to be an organ of Divine manifestations, and that whosoever allows himself to be led by the Spirit of God is the child of God, is anointed, is a Christ.

By teaching the doctrine of the anointing Holy Spirit, for the continued indwelling presence of which David prayed, Jesus did what even John the Baptist had not done. He saved mankind not only by teaching, but by living this hidden doctrine, for which he died on the cross.

The cross, revered as a symbol in pre-historic times, was first connected with the origin of fire, which, as lightning coming down from heaven in the form of a serpent, symbolised the Spirit or Word of God. For this reason, according to pre-Christian written tradition, the Word of God was represented by Moses as a fiery or brazen serpent, and was lifted up on a pole, later explained to have been a cross. In like manner the crucified Jesus was explained as the Word of God or Christ lifted up on a cross. The Mosaic and the Christian symbol connected the cross with the Word of God, the Saviour of all ages. This was done in direct connection with the ancient Eastern symbolism, which connected the cross with the origin of fire, and thus with the Divine enlightenment by the Spirit or Word of God. The origin of fire, and thus the cross, was first connected with the Pleiades and later with the sun. All this we shall prove in another place, and thus explain, in which sense St. Peter could say, that 'God anointed Jesus of Nazareth with the Holy Ghost and with power;' how St. Paul could write, that God had revealed his Son 'in' him, that Christ spoke 'in' him, that the same was also powerful 'in' the Corinthians, and that 'as many as are led by the Spirit of God are Sons (children) of God.'[1]

---

[1] Acts x. 38; Gal. i. 16; 2 Cor. xiii. 3; Rom. viii. 14.

APPENDIX.

Note I.

THE UNABBREVIATED PERIODS OF GENESIS FROM ADAM TO THE FLOOD.

If we have succeeded in proving that the so-called patriarchs before the Flood cannot be regarded as individuals, the possibility remains, that the number of years assigned to each patriarch represent successive historical periods amounting to 8225 years. Starting from the year 2360 B.C. as the year of what in Genesis is recorded as the Noachian deluge, we obtain the following list of possible historical periods.

Periods.	Number of Years.	Years B.C.
Adam	930	10,585
Seth	912	9,655
Enos	905	8,743
Cainan	910	7,838
Mahalalel	895	6,928
Jared	962	6,033
Enoch	365	5,071
Methuselah	969	4,703
Lamech	777	3,737
Noah	600	2,960
Flood	. . .	2,360

Total 8,225 years.

NOTE II.

TABLE OF HEBREW CHRONOLOGY FROM THE DEATH OF SOLOMON TO THE DESTRUCTION OF THE TEMPLE, 934–586 B.C.

B.C.	JUDAH	ISRAEL	B.C.	JUDAH	ISRAEL
934	Solomon's death		806	(36) 17 Asa (7)	15 Baasha
933	} Chaotic period		805	18	16
932		1 Jeroboam	804	19	17
931	Rehoboam (See App. note III., No. 1)		803	20	18
			802	21	19
		2	801	22	20
930	2	3	800	23	21
929	3	4	880	24	22
928	4	5	888	25	23
927	|5| 21st (20th) Shishak's (No. 2), capture of Jerusalem		887	|26|	24 |1| of Elah (8)
			886	|27|	2 |1.1| of Omri and Tibni (9)
			885	28	2
926	6	6	884	29	3
925	7	7	883	30	4
924	8	8	882	31	5
923	9	9	881	32	6
922	10	10	880	33	7
921	11	11	879	34	8
920	12	12	878	35	9
919	13	13	877	36	10
918	14	14	876	37	11
917	15	15	875	|38| 1 Jehosha-phat	12 |1| Ahab (10)
916	16	16			
915	17	17	874	39 2	2
914	18	18	873	40 3	3
913	(19) 1 of Abijam (3)	19 [(4)]	872	41 4 (1st alone, see No. 11)	|4|
912	(20) 2. |1| of Asa	|20|	871	5	5
911	(21) |2|	21 |1| Nadab (5)	870	6	6
910	(22) |3| of Asa	22 Jeroboam 2 of Nadab |1| of Baasha (6)	869	7	7
			868	8	8
			867	9	9
909	(23) 4 .	2	866	10	10
908	(24) 5 .	3	865	11	11
907	(25) 6 .	4	864	12	12
906	(26) 7 .	5	863	13	13
905	(27) 8 .	6	862	14	14
904	(28) 9 .	7	861	15	15
903	(29) 10 .	8	860	16	16
902	(30) 11 .	9	859	|17|	17 |1| Ahaziah (12)
901	(31) 12 .	10			
900	(32) 13 .	11	858	|18|	18 |1| Jehoram (13)
899	(33) 14 .	12			
898	(34) 15 .	13	857	19	(19) 2
897	(35) 16 .	14	856	20	(20) 3

APPENDIX.

B.C.	JUDAH	ISRAEL	B.C.	JUDAH	ISRAEL
855	21 Jehoshaphat	(21) Ahaziah 4 Jehoram	819	|23| Jehoash	|1| Jehoahaz (19)
|854|	22 |1| Jehoram (14)	22|5|Ahab. Jehoram. Battle on the Orontes (Karkar), according to an Assyrian inscription, against Ahab, Benhadad and others. Ahab killed in the chariot, according to the Bible, in the battle of Ramoth-Gilead.	818	24	2
			817	25	3
			816	26	4
			815	27	5
			814	28	6
			813	29	7
			812	30	8
			811	31	9
			810	32	10
			809	33	11
			808	34	12
			807	35	13
			806	36	14 [(20)
			805	|37|	(15)|1| Johoash
			804	38 |1| Amaziah (21)	(16)|2|
853	(23) 2	6	803	(39) 2	(17) 3
852	(24) 3	7	802	(40) 3	(4) 1 Jeroboam II. jointly with his father
851	(25) 4	8			
850	5	9			
849	6	10			
848	7	11	801	4	(5) 2
847	8 |1| Ahaziah (15) 1 Athaliah (17)	|12| |1| Jehu (18)	800	5	(6) 3
			799	(6) 1 Azariah(23) coregent	(7) 4
			798	(7) 2	(8) 5
846	2 Athaliah	2	797	(8) 3	(9) 6
845	3	3	796	(9) 4	(10) 7
844	4	4	795	(10) 5	(11) 8
843	5	5	794	(11) 6	(12) 9
842	6	6	793	(12) 7	(13) 10
841	7 |1| Jehoash (18)	|7|	792	(13) 8	(14) 11
			791	(14) 9	(15) 12
840	2	8	790	|15| 10	(16) 13|1| Jeroboam II. alone (22)
839	3	9			
838	4	10			
837	5	11			
836	6	12	789	(16) 11	14
835	7	13	788	(17) 12	15
834	8	14	787	(18) 13	16
833	9	15	786	(19) 14	17
832	10	16	785	(20) 15	18
831	11	17	784	(21) 16	19
830	12	18	783	(22) 17	20
829	13	19	782	(23) 18	21
828	14	20	781	(24) 19	22
827	15	21	780	(25) 20	23
826	16	22	779	(26) 21	24
825	17	23	778	(27) 22	25
824	18	24	777	(28) 23	26
823	19	25	776	(29) 24|1| Azariah or Uzziah alone (24)	|27| First Olympiad
822	20	26			
821	21	27			
820	22	28			

NOTE II.

B.C.	JUDAH	ISRAEL	B.C.	JUDAH	ISRAEL
775	25 Uzziah	28 Jeroboam II.	728	(20) [12] Ahaz.	[1] Hosea (32)
774	26	29	727	13	2
773	27	30	726	14	3
772	28	31	725	15, 1 Hezekiah	4
771	29	32		(33)	
770	30	33	724	(16) 2	5
769	31	34	723	3	6
768	32	35	722	[4]	[7]
767	33	36	721	5	8
766	34	37	720	[6] (35)	[9] Sargon
765	35	38			conquers
764	36	39			Israel
763	37	40			
762	[38]	41 [1] Zachariah	719	7	
		(25)	718	8	
		[1] of Shallum	717	9	
		(26)	716	10	
761	[39]	[1] of Menahem	715	11	
		(27)	714	12	*Contemporaneous*
			713	13	*Events.*
760	40	2	712	14	
759	41	3	711	15	First Assyrian
758	42	4			campaign to
757	43	5			Judah under
756	44	6			Sargon.
755	45	7			Merodach Ba-
754	46	8			ladan's embassy.
753	47	9	710	16	
752	48	10	709	17	Arkaianos, Sar-
751	49 (unaccounted	(11th or no reign)			gon in Baby-
	for)				lon.
750	[50]	[1] Pekahiah	708	18	
	51	(28)	707	19	
749		2	706	20	
748	[52]	[1] Pekah (20)	705	21	
747	[1] Jotham (30)	[2]	704	22	
746	2	3	703	23	
745	3	4	702	24	
744	4	5	701	25	
743	5	6	700	26	
742	6	7	699	27	
741	7	8	698	28	
740	8	9	697	(29) 1 Manasseh	
739	9 1 of Ahaz	10		(30)	
738	(10) 2	11	696	2	
737	(11) 3	12	695	3	
736	(12) 4	13	694	4	
735	(13) 5	14	693	5	
734	(14) 6	15	692	6	
733	(15) 7	16	691	7	
732	(16) 8 [1] of	[17]	690	8	
	Ahaz alone		689	9	Capture of Baby-
	(31)				lon by Senna-
					cherib.
731	(17) 9	18	688	10	
730	(18) 10	19	687	11	
729	(19) 11	20	686	12	

APPENDIX.

B.C.	Judah	Babylon	B.C.	Judah	Babylon
685	13 Manasseh		630	12 Josiah	
684	14		629	13 (44)	
683	15		628	14	
682	16		627	15	
681	17		626	16	
680	18	. . Saosdukinus	625	17	. . 1 of Nabopu-lassar
679	19				
678	20	. .	624	18	. . 2
677	21	. .	623	19	. . 3
676	22		622	20	. . 4
675	23		621	21	. . 5 Lunar eclipse recorded
674	24				
673	25		620	22	. . 6
672	26		619	23	. . 7
671	27		618	24	. . 8
670	28		617	25	. . 9
669	29		616	26	. . 10
668	30		615	27	. . 11
667	31		614	28	. . 12
666	32		613	29	. . 13
665	33		612	30	. . 14
664	34		611	31	. . 15
663	35		610	1 Jehoahaz (Shallum) (39)	16
662	36				
661	37				
660	38			1 Jehoiakim (Eliakim) (30)	
659	39				
658	40				
657	41		609	2	. . 17
656	42		608	3	. . 18
655	43		607	[4] (40)	. 10 [1] of Nebu-chadnezzar
654	44				
653	45				
652	46		606	5	. . (20) 2
651	47		605	6	. . (21) 3
650	48		604	7	. . (22) 4
649	49		603	8	. . (23) 5
648	50		602	9	. . (24) 6
647	51	. . Kineladanus	601	10	. . (25) 7
646	52		600	(11) 1 of Jehoia-chin (41) First of Captivity as computed by Ezechiel	(26) 8
645	53				
644	54				
643	(55) 1 of Amon (37)				
642	2		599	(2) 1 of Zede-kiah (42)	(27) 9
641	1 of Josiah (38)				
			598	2	(28) 10
640	2		597	3	(29) 11
639	3		596	4 ([5] of Captivity, and 30th of Nabopulassar. Ezek i. 1, 2. See No. 43)	[30] 12 (43)
638	4				
637	5				
636	6				
635	7				
634	8				
633	9				
632	10		595	5	(31) 13
631	11		594	6	(32) 14

B.C.	JUDAH		BABYLON
503	7 Zedekiah		(33) 15
502	8		(34) 16
501	9		(35) 17
500	|10|		|18| Nebuchadnezzar
589 588	⎧ 11 Zedekiah. Capture of Jerusalem (51). 12th of Captivity ⎫		19 20
587 586	⎧ Destruction of the Temple, and 1st of 70 years of Jeremiah as computed after the construction of the second Temple 516 B.C. (see p. 6). ⎫		21 22 of Nebuchadnezzar.

NOTE III.

BIBLICAL AUTHORITIES FOR THE LENGTH OF REIGNS
IN JUDAH AND ISRAEL.

OUR date for Solomon's accession, 974 B.C., is obtained by making the year 2458 B.C., that is, the date in Genesis implied for the 'birth of Shem,' the starting-point of Hebrew Chronology, and by lengthening the recorded Mosaic period of 480 years to 592 years. The same date for Solomon's accession can be obtained by reckoning backwards from the lunar eclipse in 621 B.C., the fifth of Nabopulassar, recorded by C. Ptolemy and confirmed by astronomers of our days. The 353 years from 621 to 974 B.C. form the sum total of the regnal years assigned in the Bible to the kings of Judah from (the twenty-first of) Josiah to the first of Solomon, if the last reign of a king is generally made to synchronize with the first of his successor (see Mishna-rule, p. 30), and if a system of contemporaneous reigns is adopted, which the Bible can be shown to imply. We follow Mr. Sharpe ('Chronology of the Bible,' 1868), in letting Azariah reign with his father Amaziah when sixteen years old, and from the sixth year of his father's reign:

II

thus doing away with the interregnum hitherto assumed between Jeroboam II. and his son Zachariah, who, according to the second book of Kings, began to reign in the year of his father's death. Accordingly, the twenty-seventh of Jeroboam II., synchronizes with the first of Azariah's sole regency, and likewise with the first Olympiad. We also accept Mr. Sharpe's suggested co-regency of Ahaz and Jotham until the seventeenth year of the latter, which in the Bible is mentioned as the first regnal year of the former, being, in fact, the first year of his sole regency. It is thus shown that no interregnum need be placed between Pekah and Hosea, as hitherto universally assumed.

This important discovery of Mr. Sharpe's, by which Hebrew Chronology is shown to require an abbreviation of twenty years hitherto assigned to two interregnums, is confirmed by the remarkable fact established by our Chronology, that the Biblical regnal years thus computed without any interregnum, carry us from 621 B.C. backwards to 974 as the first of Solomon, that is, precisely to the same year which we obtained by reckoning forwards the Biblical periods and regnal years from 2458 B.C. to Solomon's accession. This cannot possibly be a mere chance-coincidence. It confirms what we hope to have established on independent grounds, that the period from the Exodus to the building of the Temple extended not over 480 but over 592 years, as St. Paul and Josephus imply or assert.

We allow two years for a chaotic state after Solomon's death, in harmony with the express statements in the Septuagint, and with the implied statements of the Hebrew text about Jeroboam and Rehoboam. Our first year of Ahab synchronizes with the first year of Jehoshaphat, since the fourth of Ahab can be shown to correspond with the first of Jehoshaphat's sole regency, not of his reign. We show that the synchronism required by the Bible between the fourth of Ahab and the first of Jehoshaphat must be thus explained ; for by this interpretation of the passage in the first book of Kings, the twenty-second or last year of Ahab's reign, 854 B.C., synchronizes with the Assyrian date for the battle at Karkar on the Orontes, in which Shalmanesar II. fought against 'Ahab of Israel' and his confederates. The victory of Ahab over Benhadad at Aphek, and the covenant between these two, had preceded (probably by about three years) the battle of Karkar, which led to the dissolution of this

NOTE III. 99

confederation, to an alliance between Israel and Judah, and thus to the attack of Ramoth-Gilead, in which Ahab was mortally wounded in his chariot by a Syrian archer. Our Hebrew Chronology and the Assyrian synchronism seem to prove that the battle of Ramoth-Gilead, as well as that of Karkar, was fought in 854 B.C., this having been the last year of Ahab's reign.

To the following running numbers our preceding table of Hebrew regnal years refers.

No. (1) 1 Kings xiv. 21.
(2) 1 Kings xiv. 25; 2 Chron. xii. 2.
(3) 1 Kings xv. 1.
(4) 1 Kings xv. 9.
(5) 1 Kings xv. 25; comp. 1 Kings xiv. 20; possible co-regency.
(6) 1 Kings xv. 33.
(7) 2 Chron. xvi. 1; regnal years of Rehoboam continued.
(8) 1 Kings xvi. 8.
(9) 1 Kings xvi. 15, 22, 23.
(10) 1 Kings xvi. 29.
(11) 1 Kings xxii. 41; the first year of Jehoshaphat's sole regency is meant.
(12) 1 Kings xxii. 51; the seventeenth of Jehoshaphat's reign, not of his sole regency (comp. 1 Kings xvi. 29; xxii. 40).
(13) 2 Kings iii. 1 (disregarding 2 Kings i. 17). As Ahaziah reigned one year contemporaneously with Ahab, which is not excluded by the statement that he reigned ' in his stead,' so Ahaziah's brother Jehoram's first five regnal years synchronize with Ahab's last five.
(14) 2 Kings viii. 16, 17.
(15) 2 Kings viii. 25 (contradicting 2 Kings ix. 29).
(16) 2 Kings x. 36.
(17) 2 Kings ix. 27; xi. 4.
(18) 2 Kings xii. 1.
(19) 2 Kings xiii. 1.
(20) 2 Kings xiii. 10.
(21) 2 Kings xiv. 1, 17; xv. 1.
(22) 2 Kings xiv. 23 (see No. 24); commencement of Jeroboam's sole regency.
(23) 2 Kings xv. 2.
(24) 2 Kings xv. 1; comp. xiv. 17; Azariah twelve years co-regent with Amaziah.
(25) 2 Kings xv. 8; comp. xiv. 29, no interregnum.
(26) 2 Kings xv. 13.
(27) 2 Kings xv. 17.
(28) 2 Kings xv. 23.
(29) 2 Kings xv. 27.
(30) 2 Kings xv. 32.

100 APPENDIX.

(31) 2 Kings xvi. 1; commencement of sole reign of Ahaz.
(32) 2 Kings xvii. 1; xv. 30.
(33) 2 Kings xviii. 1 (comp. Nos. 34, 35).
(34) 2 Kings xviii. 9.
(35) 2 Kings xvii. 6; xviii. 10.
(36) 2 Kings xxi. 1.
(37) 2 Kings xxi. 19.
(38) 2 Kings xxii. i.
(39) 2 Kings xxiii. 31, 36.
(40) Jerem. xxv. 1.
(41) 2 Kings xxiv. 8–12.
(42) 2 Kings xxiv. 18.
(43) Ezek. i. 1, 2.
(44) Jerem. xxxii. 1.

Note IV.
DATE OF THE ACCESSION OF THOTHMES THE GREAT.
(By Mr. Basil H. Cooper.)

I PURPOSE to give a revised *résumé* of my Astronomical Proof that Thothmes III. reckoned his accession from B.C. 1515.[1] The proof is based on the combination of a Sothiac or Dogstar Rising Date with a New Moon Date, both recorded on inscriptions of Thothmes the Great.

In 1860 I accepted the inference of Lepsius, Brugsch, Birch, and others, that the Elephantiné Festival Tablet, containing the entry, 'Rising of the Dogstar on the 28th of Epiphi,' must be a monument of that king, because *débris* bearing his scutcheons were found close by. I now know that the Festival Tablet itself mentions him by name; as the offerer and celebrant at these festivals, one of which is this of the Rising of Sirius, the *dies solennis* for which amongst the Egyptians all the evidence, classical and epigraphical, proves to have been the 20th of July, or more strictly speaking, the Egyptian day which began with the morning of the 19th and ended with that of the 20th. In the imbissextile kalendar of the First Sothiac Period, that of Arnimos,[2] which began with the Rising of

---

[1] *British Quart. Rev.* Oct. 1860, art., 'Egyptology and the Two Exodes'; reprinted under the title, 'Hieroglyphical Date of the Exodus,' by B. H. Cooper, 1861.

[2] So Censorinus (*De Die Nat.* c. 19) and the monuments name the Pharaoh who first added the Five Days of the Epact at the end of the twelve months of Thirty Days each, which made up the Primitive Egyptian Year,

NOTE IV.

Sirius on the Egyptian New Year's Day = 20th July, B.C. 2783, the 28th of Epiphi answered to the 20th of July during the single tetraëteris B.C. 1477-4. It follows that one of the above four years B.C. 1477, 1476, 1475, or 1474 must have fallen within the reign of Thothmes the Great.

Lepsius was perfectly aware of the cogency of this inference, and since it did not accord with his identification of the Menophres, under whom the astronomer Theon made the Second Sothiac Period begin B.C. 1323, with Menephtha, son of Ramses II. Sesostris, he supposed that the stonecutter must have blunderingly put Epiphi for the preceding month Payni. This pushed up the astronomical coincidence, which Lepsius has always loyally held to belong to Thothmes III., just 30 × 4 or 120 years. He had inherited that identification from Champollion-Figeac, whose decided genius for chronology had seized on this fragment of Theon, and on a statement in the Syncelline Canon (the so-called 'Sothis Book'), that the Hykshos Conquest took place in the 700th year of the Sothiac Period, as the two main pillars of his system. The name most like Menophres to be found in the Manethonian lists was that of the son of Ramses-Sesostris, viz. Menephthes, whilst the forename of the grandfather of Sesostris, Ramses I., of which Menophres is an exact transcript, used to figure in the books as 'Men * * Ra' many years after the younger Champollion was laid beneath his obelisk in Père La Chaise. It was in the 'Dublin University Magazine' for July 1859, and not long after the discovery of the phonetic value of the previously unknown sign[1] in the half-deciphered name, which every

a reform which could have taken place only at the beginning of a Sothiac Period. This very significant name Arnimos, *i.e.* 'Horus,' the Sun and Year god, 'Regenerated,' belongs to Amenemha I., and is not known to have been borne by any other Pharaoh save Seti I., who, as appears from an inscription at Paris, was already reigning along with his father, Menophres Ramses I., when the *Second* Sothiac Period began, B.C. 1323. Amenemha I. reformed the Egyptian Kalendar in his 21st year, B.C. 2783, when he associated his son, Osortsen I., with himself in the kingdom. The Five Days of the Epact never appear on the monuments before this time, but already in the reign of Osortsen I. they are several times mentioned. Fruin reads Amenemes for the corrupt Arminos in Censorinus, which comes to the same thing. Solely on paleographical grounds I prefer the above emendation.

[1] Dr. Birch was the discoverer. The lamented Vicomte de Rougé, in his 'Mémoire sur l'Inscription du Tombeau d'Anhmes,' which first appeared

Egyptian scholar can now read Men-peh-Ra, that Dr. Hincks announced his identification of this king with Theon's Menophres. The important correction was unhappily too late to influence Lepsius, whose 'Königsbuch' was published in 1858. The substitution of Ramses I. for Menephtha, as the Menophres of the Era would have given him exactly the 120 years which he was obliged to charge to the account of the blundering stonecutter, ridding him at one stroke of the necessity for arbitrarily altering either the hieroglyphical date or the Greek name in Theon's text. As Professor Eisenlohr well observes, Theon's Pharaoh Menophres bears a name involving that of the Sungod Ra, which appears in almost every Egyptian royal name, whilst in Menephtha the divine name is that of Ra's father Phtha, the Egyptian Hephaistos. In other words, the names Menephthes and Menophres both bear the genuine Egyptian stamp. At the same time they are perfectly distinct.

Moreover, had the successors of Champollion-Figeac loyally rallied to the important reform proposed by the very learned and acute Dr. Hincks, they would have been better prepared to do justice to the other astronomical date, which, together with the misinterpreted fragment of Theon, induced the very able French chronologist to make Sirius his guiding star through the labyrinth of the Egyptian annals. They would then have seen how unwise it was to throw away the invaluable date of the Hykshos Conquest, the 700th year of the Sothiac Period, merely on account of the tainted source whence it comes. Of course the forger would be sure to trick out his imposture with such notorious truisms as this genuine popular date with its round number of years must have been in Egypt, even down to the fifth century, when his patchwork system of Egyptian chronology from Menes-Mizraim to Alexander the Great was first published there as the 'genuine' work of Manetho. The title, 'Sothis,' or, 'The Dogstar,' as the Egyptian word means, pitched on by the dishonest monk for his fabrication, sufficiently indicates that this was precisely the sort of bait

in the *Mémoires* of the French Academy of Inscriptions and Belles Lettres in 1853, was still unconvinced of the truth of the new reading (p. 146). I am indebted for this reference to Mr. Lapage Renouf, whose immense stores of erudition are always at the service of his fellow Egyptists.

he held out to make his wares pass current. Even before the discovery of the art of printing, every peasant in our island must have had some dim idea of the date of the Norman Conquest, if no other ray of English chronology had ever found its way into his poor dark brain. So in Egypt, until the memory of the earlier Foreign Conquest was blotted out by the later horrors perpetrated by Omar and his hordes, the poorest Copt must have retained some notion as to his nation having once dated events by a Sothiac Era, about the 700th year of which the children of Shem under Salatis made themselves lords of Egypt. Very possibly they knew no better than the author[1] of the pious fraud called the 'Sothis' when the Dog-star Period began.

With Hincks's correction of Champollion-Figeac's premature identification of Menophres, the French scholar's two astronomical dates, together with Lepsius's Sothiac date of Thothmes the Great, just as the stonecutter left it, for a third, are as harmonious as the Three Graces.

Of the agreement of the Menophres Era, as explained by Dr. Hincks, with the Elephantiné inscription, I have already spoken. Nor is it less clear that if Ramses I., the last king of Dyn. XVIII., be Menophres, the Hykshos must have conquered Egypt according to Manetho, as well as the 'Sothis,' about the 700th year of the First Sothiac Period. For Josephus gives us a Manethonian Total of 393 years from their Expulsion by Amasis to the end of Dyn. XIX., of which 140 years come after Menophres Ramses. There remain 253, which, added to the 511 of the Hykshos Occupation = 764. Hence they came in 764 years before Menophres, or in other words, in the year of the First Sothiac Period, 1461 — 764 or 697. The same year of the Sothiac Period, 697, results from adding together the 213 years assigned in the Turin Papyrus to the Twelfth Dynasty, from the Association of Amenemes I. and his son Osortsen I., and the 484 of the Xoite Dynasty in Lower Egypt,

[1] Perhaps we should rather say the author's younger contemporary and editor, Anianus, a monk also, but a far less learned one than the probable author, Panodorus, who, though very dishonest, seems to have been anything but an ignoramus. Anianus very likely lowered the starting-point of the List of Kings about half a century, to fit his own date of the Dispersion of Noah's Grandchildren. The original author, like Herr von Gumpach in our own day, dated the accession of Menes in the first year of the Sothiac Period next before that of Menophres.

down to the Hykshos Conquest, which its long struggle with the rival Theban Kings naturally rendered so easy.

I do think it is deeply to be regretted that of the elder Champollion's two key-dates, his successors not only threw away the precious and retained the vile, but by so doing compelled themselves to treat their own still more valuable contribution, the Sothiac block of Elephantiné, in a perfectly arbitrary manner. Thus only can it be explained that after twenty years' further laborious research, crowned with success in every other department, men still complain, as Fanny Corbaux did in 1855, that we are floundering about in a gulf of four centuries, unable to moor a date of even Ramses III. to any fixed year B.C. within that enormous range.

Unfortunately I was not myself aware in 1860 of the immense stride in advance taken shortly before by Dr. Hincks. How wonderfully it simplifies the case, especially with the help of the Stela of Amenemheb, an old campaigner under Thothmes himself, just discovered by Dr. Ebers,[1] we shall at once see.

We now know, from this inscription, that Thothmes III. reigned from the 4th of Pachom[2] in his first year till his death on the 30th of Phamenoth, in his fifty-fourth. Moreover, the New Moon Date in his Annals at Karnak—viz. the 21st (not 22nd, as formerly misread) of Pachom, in his twenty-third year, the anniversary of his coronation, and the day on which he fought the important battle which ended with the taking of Megiddo, is at last clear of all difficulties. The text is now happily quite safe, which had been falsely copied in the standard transcripts, the new moon group having been left unrecognisable even by such experts as Dr. Birch. Another gain in the interval is that this Feria of the New Moon here is no longer an isolated and so far incomprehensible case. We have now the complete list of the Thirty Lunar Feriæ, each of which had its name, like our days of the week, and its tutelary god. We now know too that the ancient Egyptians, somewhat like

[1] See the *Zeitschrift* of Lepsius and Brugsch for January and February 1873, for the text of this new and invaluable historical document, with a complete German translation.

[2] This date is clearly given as that of the King's accession in a contemporary Karnak Festival List. On this day also, in his 'Annals,' his regnal years are found to change. The day of his death we first learn from the new Stela of Ebers.

the modern Jews, reckoned *two* New Moon Feriæ in each Lunar Month, the former being the day of the conjunction and the latter the day of the phase. All these lunar *feriæ* were cyclically fixed, not by observation *pro re nata*, but according to a system so exact that whenever these *feriæ* occur combined with other kalendarial dates, they are always to be regarded as astronomical notes of time of the very highest value. I have found them so occurring under the Twelfth Dynasty, and even under the Sixth. The New Moon with which I am here concerned is the Dark or Astronomical New Moon, which in B.C. 1493 coincided with the 21st of Pachom=May 17-18 in that year. The conjunction fell about noon on May 17th. Supposing this to be the Pharaoh's twenty-third year, his first was of course B.C. 1515. Doubtless in the abstract there are alternative dates, but practically there is not one. The Lunar Cycle of the Imbissextile or Vague Egyptian Kalendar of exactly 365 days is twenty-five years, with an error of little more than an hour. Hence the lunar conjunction took place also on the 21st of Pachom, B.C. 1493+25=B.C. 1518. But to make this the king's twenty-third year is to make his first B.C. 1540, between which and B.C. 1477, the very earliest of the four consecutive years when the 28th of Epiphi coincided with the 20th of July, as the inscription records was the case when he presented his offerings at Elephantiné, are sixty-three years, whereas he reigned, as the Ebers Stela records, but fifty-four. Moreover, like the lower alternative B.C. 1494-25= B.C. 1469, this hypothesis would rob us of what we cannot afford and do not mean to lose. I refer to the beautiful harmony which we attain by means of the intermediate date May 17-18 B.C. 1493 with the Era of Menophres. If Thothmes III. began to reign B.C. 1515, then his fifty-four years end B.C. 1461, between which and the Era of Menophres, or the beginning of the Second Sothiac Period on the Egyptian New Year's Day, the first of Thoth=July 19-20th B.C. 1323, are 138 years. But this is precisely the sum of the reigns which Manetho interposes between his Mēsphra-Tuthmosis (Men-sheper-Ra Thothmes III.) and Menophres Ramses I. I rectify in Josephus, with the monuments and Syncellus, the transposition of Aai-sphres[1]

---

[1] For the corrupt ΜΙΣΦΡΙΣ, of the Lists, I read ΑΑΙΣΦΡΗΣ. Of course Armaïs, in like manner, reigns after his father, Menophres Ramses I., not

(Aai-sheperu-Ra, the forename of the son and successor of Thothmes III.—viz. Amen-hotep II.). For Rathos (Manetho's rightly-read name of the son-in-law and successor of the Disk-worshipper Ach-n-atn-Ra, the Achenchethres of Manetho) I read five years and nine months, instead of nine years, in accord with the six years in Africanus. Lastly, I restore, with the monuments, the dropped unit five to the reign of Amenophthis III. These are all the changes I allow myself in Manetho's numbers as reported by our oldest authority, Josephus. The result is a total, including the single year and four months of Menophres Ramses himself, of 138 years and six months.

The reciprocal verification leaves nothing to be desired. The Era falls critically within the short reign of sixteen months assigned by Manetho to Menophres Ramses I. I submit, therefore, that the reign of Thothmes the Great, the Conqueror of Syria and Mesopotamia, is determined with at least as great a degree of certainty as that of Alexander, and with even greater precision. He ascended the throne of the Pharaohs May 7th, B.C. 1515, and vacated it by his death March 21st, B.C. 1461.

NOTE V.

SHISHAK I. AND PSUSENNES II. CO-REGENTS.

(BY MR. BASIL H. COOPER.)

a. THE fact, long since demonstrated by Lepsius, from the inscriptions on the statue of the Nile-god dedicated by Prince Shishak, son of Osorkon I. (Dyn. xxii. 2), and grandson of the conqueror of Rehoboam, that this prince was at the same time the grandson, on the mother's side, of Psusennes II., seems to warrant the inference that the two grandfathers belonged to one and the same generation, *i.e.* that the reigns of Psusennes II. and Shishak I. were, in part at least, contemporaneous.

before him, as in the present text. His name has not yet been found on the monuments, but his forename has turned up in the Serapeum. An Apis died under him. Mariette places it next to the second of the two which died under Horus, and before that which iod nder Seti I., the brother of Armais.

b. This surmise is strongly corroborated when we compare the remarkable variations in the Manethonian fragments as to the lengths of the respective reigns. The Eusebian tradition of Manetho's numbers assigns to Psusennes thirty-five years; and these are necessary to complete the total of 130 years for the dynasty, which not only Eusebius but Africanus also assigns to these Tanite kings. Yet Africanus, confessedly the more trustworthy of the two, gives this king no more than fourteen years, at the cost of a want of harmony between his total and his details. No emending pen finer than a house-painter's brush can possibly reconcile these numerals. Neither of them can be the blunder of a scribe, but they imply *different points of view.* Manetho must have said that this king reigned fourteen years, and Manetho must have said that he reigned thirty-four.

Accordingly, we find an exactly *complementary* double tradition as to the length of the reign of Shishak I. Eusebius and Africanus agree in reporting that he reigned twenty-one years, but in the Syncelline Canon (the 'Sothis') he has thirty-four. There may have been authority for the statement that he reigned thirty-four years, and there is the best authority for the statement that he reigned but twenty-one. I submit, in anticipating an objection from the notorious bad faith of the Pseudo-Manethonian 'Sothis,' that the appearance of a variant number in that tainted Canon alone ought not *eo ipso* to put it out of court. At the same time I readily own that the evidence of a witness of this calibre is not to be lightly trusted without corroboration. But I contend that in this instance the striking variation is abundantly confirmed, both by a comparison of the traditional numbers between themselves, and, what weighs infinitely more, by the monumental indications. The 'thirty-five' and 'fourteen' for Psusennes II., and the 'thirty-four' and 'twenty-one' for Shishak I., point to their having been rival sovereigns for thirteen years, and to their then having made up their differences by an intermarriage between the two royal houses; which event the Bubastite, now first recognised by the Legitimist Manetho, survived twenty-one years, and the Tanite twenty-two. I now come to the monumental confirmation of this view, which I treat separately on account of its great importance.

c. Vicomte de Rougé long since called attention to the historical importance of the Banner Name of Shishak I., 'Crowned to unite the Upper and the Lower Countries.' This implies a previous period of antagonism between Upper and Lower Egypt, and its termination by some political arrangement symbolised by the recognition and coronation of the Bubastite Pharaoh.

d. Again, in the Silsilis inscription, dated Payni 1st, in his twenty-first year, it is said of Shishak I. that 'Ammon Ra has set him on the throne in order to finish what he began when he took the government of Egypt *for the second time.*' Here a twofold, if not a threefold reckoning of the reign of the head of the Bubastite house is affirmed by a contemporary monument.

e. Still stronger, and indeed, in my view, conclusive of the question, is the testimony of the inscriptions on the back of the Nile-god statue already referred to. The Prince Shishak, who erected the monument, is thereon called the son of the marriage between the first Bubastite's son and next successor Osorkon I. and Rakamat, daughter of Psusennes II.; and, as already observed by Brugsch and others, both Psusennes II. and Osorkon I. there appear *as living and reigning together.* The statue is in the British Museum, and I again inspected it carefully the other day in company with its custodian, Dr. Birch, the most accomplished Egyptist in the world; and both of us were entirely agreed that there is not the slightest trace of the mortuary epithet 'Osirian,' or of the analogous term 'justified,' ever having been appended to either royal ring, as would almost infallibly have been the case had either been dead when the inscription was cut. The inference is irresistible. The date of the statue is the thirty-sixth current, but probably never completed, of Psusennes II., running parallel with the first of his son-in-law, Osorkon I., whose father, Shishak I., the young Prince Shishak's maternal grandfather, must have survived a whole twelvemonth. This is in exact accord with the literary tradition, that Psusennes II. reigned 'fourteen' years (viz. before the political marriage), and that he reigned 'thirty-five' (having survived that marriage twenty-one); further, that Shishak I. reigned 'thirty-four' years (viz. from his disputing the succession with Psusennes II.), but that he did not reign more than 'twenty-one,' dating from the treaty, of which the political marriage was the symbol.

I am happy to be able to add, that, having read this note to Dr. Birch, he authorises me to say he endorses my statement of the monumental facts, and deems my inferences from them reasonable.

Note VI.
ON DEIOKES AND DAIUCCU.
(By Mr. Sayce.)

The name of the *Mannian* (or Minnian) chief Daiuccu, who was transported to Hamath by Sargon in 715, shows no more than that the name Deiokes was a possible one among the Medes and their linguistically related neighbours in the 8th century B.C. But it may be possible to detect the Deiokes of Herodotus in a name which occurs in the account of a later campaign of Sargon—somewhere about 714 or 713 B.C.—against certain countries in the North-East. These are Ellibi, Karalla, and *Bit-Daiuccu*. Now as the names of the kings of the other countries are given, it appears very likely (as Lenormant has pointed out) that no monarch of Bit-Daiuccu is mentioned, because Daiuccu was still on the throne. If Lenormant (followed by Finzi) is right in identifying Ellibi with Ekbatana, Deiokes would not have become master of that part of Media until after B.C. 702, when Sennacherib came into conflict with Ispabara (? 'Αστιβαρας), who had been placed upon the throne of Ellibi by Sargon in B.C. 709, in preference to his brother Nibe, after the death of their father Dalta or Rita (compare 'Αρταῖος; the first character may be read either *dal* or *ri*). Now, according to Diodorus (II. 30), Ktesias —a very suspicious authority, certainly—stated that Aspadas was called Astyages by the Greeks; and I cannot help thinking that in the Greek accounts of both Deiokes and Astyages we have a confusion of the mythical Azi-daháka and his exploits with an historical Dai-uccu. It is very possible that Dai-uccu not only recovered himself after Sargon's expedition, but extended his dominions, and furthered Nibe's pretensions after Dalta's death, thus occasioning Sargon's interference in Ellibi. His rise might thus be placed B.C. 711. As regards the name which Schrader and Lenormant write Dajaukku and Dayaukku, the last double consonant is *caph*, while the preceding characters should always be read *dai*, not *daya*. It forms Gentile nouns in Assyrian.

NOTE VII.
MURDER OF JOSHUA AND ZECHARIAH.

THE murder of 'a certain Joshua' by his 'brother' (in office?) the high priest Johannan, according to a tradition transmitted by Josephus (Ant. xi. 7), can be connected with the high-priest Joshua and his antagonist, adversary, or 'Satan,' to which one of the visions of Zechariah refers, and which we have connected with the year 518-517 B.C. For it is probable that Bagoses kept his promise and helped to procure for Joshua the highpriesthood. At that very exceptional time a second highpriest may well have been appointed, if the two lines of Aaronites in Israel, called after Eleazar and Ithamar, have been by us with sufficient reason connected respectively with the tribes of Benjamin and of Judah.[1] We have shown that 'the stranger' in Israel, the Kenite or Rechabite, in the time of Joshua settled in Arad with the tribe of Judah, that Thamar is by Philo called 'the stranger,' that the story of Judah's marriage with her may by the matrimonial metaphor be explained as referring to the national union between Hebrews and strangers, and that the line of Ithamar seems to refer to a highpriestly line of the stranger in Israel, of the Kenites to which Jethro belonged, and with which the Rechabites are ethnically connected. To the Rechabites, who had always been 'strangers' in Israel, but who nevertheless worshipped in the temple, and some of whose names are compounded with the name of Jehovah, Jeremia promised in the name of Jehovah-Zabaot a never-ceasing priesthood, and even a high priesthood, inasmuch as 'to stand before' God is an ex-

[1] *The Keys of St. Peter, or the History of Rechab*; comp. *Die Einheit der Religionen*, i.

pression referring to the highpriest in the Holiest of the Holy (Jer. xxxv. 18, 19.)

As Jethro 'the Kenite' or Rechabite, like Melchizedek, was a priest of the highest God, and yet a Non-Hebrew, the priesthood of Jethro and therefore also the priesthood promised to the sons of Rechab, the descendants of Jonadab, possibly a brother of David, might be called a priesthood 'after the order of Melchizedek.' This leads us to assume that the 110th Psalm may have been written by one of the Rechabites, of whom we are told that they followed the Hebrews into exile, and that this Psalm refers to the promise made by Divine command to Jonadab, the patriarch and Lord of the Rechabites, whose injunctions they had so obediently followed, that Jeremiah pointed them out as patterns to Israel. The promised Messiah was to be a son of David, who descended from the Kenites that came from Hamath, so that, like David, the Messiah was to be a Non-Hebrew, a stranger in Israel. Melchizedek, the Non-Hebrew, is pointed out in Holy Writ as the type of the Messiah, of Jesus of Nazareth. Thus the connection is confirmed between the priesthood after the order of Melchizedek, and the stranger 'within the gates' of Israel.

This second priesthood of the stranger in Israel, with which the Aaronic line of Ithamar seems to have been connected, occupied the highpriestly office in the time of Eli and his successors before Zadok (1148-774 B.C.), but it cannot be proved that any highpriest after Zadok, who was of the line of Eleazar, belonged to the line of Ithamar. Although the line of Ithamar did occupy the highpriestly chair, the succession of the line of Ithamar is omitted in the Chronicles (1 Chron. vi. 3-12 ; xxiv. 2-6), and yet the succession of the line of Eleazar is twice recorded. Moreover in that part of the book of Ezekiel which refers to the new temple, reference is made to a Divine command, that the sons of Zadok only, no other Aaronites than those of the line of Eleazar, should 'stand before' God, that is, appear as highpriests in the Holiest of the Holy (Ezek. xliv. 9-31). This command excludes the promise made by the prophet Jeremiah to the sons of Jonadab, the Rechabites or strangers, that Jonadab the son of Rechab shall not want a man to 'stand before' God 'for ever.'

Yet in the same book which bears the name of the prophet

Ezekiel, and directly connected with the above-quoted passage (Ezek. xliv. 7, 8), the fact is acknowledged and condemned, that at the time of the return from Babylon, and therefore at the time of the temple of Serubbabel in which Joshua officiated, Israel has brought into the sanctuary 'strangers, uncircumcised in the heart and uncircumcised in the flesh,' that they might be in God's sanctuary 'to pollute it.' The true Israel, according to the book of Ezekiel, ought not to have allowed strangers to be keepers of God's charge in the sanctuary. The true Israel, according to the book of Jeremiah, could not have done better than to appoint strangers in Israel to stand before God in the Holiest of the Holy. The fulfilment of the prophecy of Jeremiah is condemned by the prophet Ezekiel, although the prophet Zechariah sanctioned everything that was done by Serubbabel and Joshua, whilst referring to the adversary or Satan who 'stood before' the Angel of Jehovah at the right hand of Joshua 'to resist him' or 'to accuse him.' Perhaps the 109th Psalm refers to Joshua and his adversary, the 84th to Joshua 'the anointed.'

We may now assert, that in the year to which that vision of Zechariah refers, 518-517 B.C., two highpriests officiated at Jerusalem, that is, Joshua, who probably belonged to the line of Ithamar, and another highpriest, the adversary of Joshua, of the hostile line of Eleazar. If we have shown that the murder in the temple of 'a certain Joshua' by his 'brother' (in office) the highpriest Johannan may be connected with the highpriest Joshua and his adversary, who with him stood before the Lord in the Holiest of the Holy, the adversary of Joshua may be identified with the highpriest Johannan, the murderer of Joshua the highpriest.

In the works referred to, in which the first attempt has been made to sketch out the ethnic relations and the history of the stranger in Israel, we believe to have proved conclusively, that the first highpriest after the return from Babylon, that Joshua, was the grandson and successor of the high priest Seraja, whom Nebukadnezzar caused to be slain at Riblah, and that Seraja's predecessor was Azariah, which name has the same meaning as Eleazar, so that one name could be used instead of the other. This highpriest Joshua seems to have been the reviser of the 'Proverbs' or 'Wisdom of Sirach,' the original of which was written in Hebrew. The name Sirach is in ancient manuscripts written Seirach, and may be identified with Seraja the highpriest. In the prologue to the Apocrypha called Jesus Sirach or Ecclesiasticus, which prologue has probably been worked over at a later time in the form we possess it, Jesus or Joshua is called the son of Seirach, and in the book itself is connected with its authorship, and is called Jesus the son of Sirach 'of Jerusalem,' whereby our identification of Sirach with Seraja the high priest of Jerusalem is confirmed.

It is said of this Sirach, that he had collected, not that he published, 'grave and short sentences of wise men that had been before him,' and that he 'himself also added some of his own, full of understanding and of wisdom.' St. Jerome knew the Hebrew original of this Apocrypha, and Athanasius says, that it had been framed by 'the fathers, to be read by those who wish to be instructed in the word of godliness.' Thus the identification of Sirach and Seraja gains in force, for such collections of traditional lore, particularly if not intended for the use of all, would be made by or with the authority of the highpriest, in times when the word of the interpreter or Targumist was held in higher reverence than the Scriptures.

It is of no importance whether the Greek translator of the collection of Sirach lived in the time of the first or of the second of the Ptolemies, and whether his name was likewise Jesus or Joshua. As Joshua or Jesus was the son of 'Sirach of Jerusalem,' so the latter is in ancient manuscripts called 'the son of Eleazar,' and in the Talmud likewise 'Jeshoshua ben Sira ben Elieser.' As we may substitute Azariah for Eleazar, the ancient and probably the original title of Ecclesiasticus referred to the names of three successive highpriests, to Azariah of the time of Jehojakim (since 610 B.C.), of Seraja the contemporary of Zedekiah (since 599), and of Joshua the contemporary of Serubbabel (since 536). The son of Seraja, and father of Joshua, was Jehozadak, who was transported to Babylon (1 Chron. vi. 15). Seraja the highpriest, son of Eleazar or Azariah the highpriest, collected the oracles of tradition, which by the son of Seraja, by Jehozadak, were safely kept, and by his son the highpriest Joshua were revised and, perhaps, amplified.

A welcome light is thus thrown on the origin and authority of 'the secret rolls,' the 'megillath setharim,' the Genûsim or

APPENDIX.

Apocrypha, writings containing wisdom of the initiated, secret tradition or 'hidden wisdom.' Such writings were composed by or with the sanction of the highest ecclesiastical authorities. What is now proved of the book of Ecclesiasticus may also be safely asserted with regard to the other Apocrypha the 'Wisdom of Solomon.' Since the predecessor of Azariah, to whom Seraja succeeded, was Hilkiah the highpriest and contemporary of Jeremiah, if not his father, and as he found in the temple 'the book of the law of Jehovah (as given) by Moses,' which was unknown to Hilkiah, to Huldah the prophetess, to Josiah, and the elders, but at once acknowledged as containing words of God, we may connect the proverbs of Sirach-Seraja with the discovery of this document, which was made five years before Jeremiah's being acknowledged as a prophet, that is, in the eighteenth year of Josiah, 624 B.C. This not improbable connection is all the more important, because Hilkiah, father of Jeremiah, was a priest of Anatoth in the land of Benjamin, and since Anatoth in the time of Joshua and of Solomon belonged to the Aaronites of the house of Ithamar (Jos. xxi. 18; 1 Kings ii. 26). Two of the most learned fathers of the Church, the Alexandrian Clement and St. Jerome, have identified Hilkiah the father of Jeremiah with Hilkiah the highpriest. We may, therefore, now assert, that since in no instance it can be proved that any possessions of Aaronites became alienated from them, the line of Ithamar, to which Anatoth belonged, occupied the highpriesthood in the time of Hilkiah the priest of Anatoth. This being proved, it is equally certain that the highpriests Seraja and Joshua belonged to this Aaronic line which we have connected with the strangers or Rechabites to whom Jeremiah the son of Hilkiah promised in the name of God an eternal priesthood.

It becomes more and more probable that the 110th Psalm, referring to this priesthood of the stranger in Israel under the name of a priesthood after the order or manner of Melchizedek, was composed by one of these strangers or Rechabites, whom Jeremiah extolled. As Joshua is now proved to have been connected with the line of Ithamar, and therefore probably was a Rechabite, it is reasonable to assume that the 110th Psalm, referring to the fulfilment of Jeremiah's prophecy by the elevation of Joshua to the highpriesthood, was composed in the time of Joshua, if not by himself.

APPENDIX. 115

A direct connection is now established between one of the most important Apocrypha of the Septuagint, published between the second and the third century before the Christian era, and 'Parables of Knowledge' or 'Treasures of Wisdom' (Ecclus. i. 25), that is, oracles of tradition transmitted in writing by highpriests before and immediately after the Babylonian captivity. The expression of enmity contained in the last chapter of Ecclesiasticus (l. 25, 26) against the Samaritans, the Philistines, and the people in Sichem occurs after the mention of the highpriest Simon the Just (Zadok, 391 ?–348), and cannot be attributed to the highpriest Seraja or to Joshua. The essential and more developed doctrines of the Apocrypha contain a protest against the known doctrines of the Sadducees, especially against their non-belief in Angels or spirits, and the future life, also against their separatist principles as exemplified and acted upon by Ezra. The doctrines about the word or power or spirit of God saving the souls of mankind 'in all ages,' being the universal 'Saviour,' are directly connected with the teachings of Jesus and the apostles; they form the connecting link between the Old and the New Testament.

Before we proceed, we recapitulate the main points of our investigation. In the year 536 Joshua was appointed highpriest at Jerusalem, and in 516 he consecrated the temple. He was the contemporary of Cyrus, Serubbabel, Cambyses, Hystaspes, and Bagoses. The latter had promised and procured to Joshua the highpriesthood, who had a brother in office, the highpriest Johannan. Whilst both were in the temple Johannan murdered Joshua. This took place in 516 or soon after, Joshua and Serubbabel being last mentioned in 516, the year before Ezra's mission to Jerusalem. Already in 518 Zechariah refers to an adversary of Joshua's standing at his right hand in the Holiest of the Holy, and Ezekiel refers to the appointment of strangers in the second temple, even to the stranger standing before God as highpriest.

The highpriest Joshua was a descendant from Seraja, Azariah, and Hilkiah, the priest of Anatoth, in the possession of the line of Ithamar, which was connected with the continued priesthood promised by Hilkiah's son to the Rechabites or strangers, and to which the 110th Psalm refers as to a priesthood after the order or manner of Melchizedek. Like Melchizedek, Jethro, and David, Joshua was a stranger in Israel. So was Serubbabel, a descendant of the Royal house of Judah. Serubbabel and Joshua were pointed out as God's chosen instruments by Zechariah the prophet, who was the son of Berechaiah. A son of Serubbabel was called Berechaiah (1 Chr. iii. 20), and therefore was likewise a descendant from David, the Kenite, Rechabite, or stranger.[1] We may therefore assume, that Zechariah's father Berechaiah was likewise a stranger in Israel. Joshua, Serubbabel, and Zechariah being strangers, must have encouraged the participation of the Samaritans in the building of the new temple, and likewise the marriages of Hebrews with strangers. Yet none of these are mentioned among those who on this account were banished by Ezra in 515. The natural presumption is, that they had ceased to live between 516 and 515 (514), nor is any of them mentioned after this time.

If the murder of Joshua in the temple took place in 516-515, just before or after Ezra's arrival at Jerusalem with power over life and death, it is not likely that either Serubbabel or Zechariah was spared. Indeed we have now every reason to consider the prophet Zechariah, son of Berechaiah, as the Zechariah, son of Berechaiah, to whom Jesus refers as having been murdered between the temple and the altar (Mat. xxiii. 29-36). This reference is made in an address which is directly connected with 'the blood of the prophets,' and in which the Scribes and Pharisees are called 'children of them which killed the prophets.' The murder of Joshua the highpriest, and probably also that of Zechariah the prophet, having taken place about the time when Ezra banished all those who had married strange wives, including Aaronites, the taking of Jerusalem by Bagoses, to which Josephus refers, seems to have taken place during the short and abruptly ended governorship of Ezra in 515. If Ezra remained in Jerusalem during this attack—which is most likely —he will have been put to death by Bagoses, just as the highpriest Seraja was put to death by Nebukadnezzar after the siege of Jerusalem. This assumption is confirmed by the mysterious fact, that Ezra is not mentioned a few months after his arrival at Jerusalem as governor.

[1] About David's descent see *Keys of St. Peter*, and *Einheit der Religionen*, i., 229.

APPENDIX. 117

According to the statement of Josephus, Bagoses punished the Jews for the murder of Joshua by imposing on them a tribute to be paid during seven years. It can be proved that this important event took place before Nehemiah was appointed governor. For it is stated at the commencement of the book of Nehemiah, that in the 20th year of the reign of 'Artaxerxes,' that is, of the 'king of the Aryans,' Hystaspes—therefore in the year 502—one of Nehemiah's brethren, Hanani, with several men of Judah came to Nehemiah in the palace of Shushan, when the royal cupbearer 'asked them concerning the Jews that had escaped, which were left of the captivity, and concerning Jerusalem.' The reply was, 'The remnant that are left of the captivity there in the province are in great affliction and reproach, the wall of Jerusalem also is broken down, and the gates thereof are burned with fire.' To the same time refers the 80th Psalm, where reference is made to the walls of Jerusalem being broken down and burnt with fire (13, 17). Thus the Alexandrian tradition is confirmed, according to which this Psalm was composed during the Assyrian rule.

We may now assert, that the attack on Jerusalem was made by Bagoses in the year 515, and that it put an end to the embassy of Ezra, and probably to his life. The consequence of this must have been an increased influence of the stranger at Jerusalem, and thus of the party of the stranger in Israel. Ezra's attempt to put an end to that influence might have led, under the protection of Bagoses in Samaria and Haman at Babylon, to an attempt to destroy the influence of the Hebrew party opposed to the stranger by a wholesale massacre, such as is more or less poetically described in the book of Esther. The beauty of this Benjamite played an important part in the palace intrigue, by which Mordechai was appointed in the place of Haman. The new policy ensuing on this change of ministers saved the Hebrew party at Jerusalem, and the feast of Purim was instituted on the 14th and 15th Adar (Nisan) of the 12th year of Ahasuerus or Darius Hystaspes—thus in the year 510, only a few months before the seven years of tribute were over which Bagoses had imposed at the end of Ezra's mission. The first Purim-feast took place 2,383 years ago.

INDEX.

AAI

AAI-SPHRES (Aai-shoporu-Ra), reign of, 105
Aaronites, two lines of, in Israel, 110
Abraham, date of, 2
— date of his exodus from Haran, 11, 13. His return from Egypt to Canaan, and defeat of Chedorlaomer, King of Elam, at Shiddim, 12, 84. His ancestors and their dwelling-place, 16. Reason why he was kindly received by the Hyksos-Pharaoh, 18. Assisted by the Egyptians in the expulsion of Chedorlaomer, 18, 19. Regarded as an Aryan or Japhetite chief, whose ancestors had first come to Shinar from the East, 23. Would be welcomed by the Hyksos of Egypt, 23. Reasons for this, 23
Ach-n-atn-Ra, reign of, 106
Actium, the Egyptian era of the battle of, 68
Adam, date of, 2. His age when he begat Seth, 4. Time required intervening between the Flood and the creation of, 7. Recorded dwelling-place of the first descendants of, 17. Possible historical period represented by, 22
Africanus, or Julius the African, priest or bishop of Emmaus-Nicopolis in Judæa, his trustworthy chronology, 52. Number of years which he gives for the reign of the nineteenth dynasty, 55
Ahab, King of Israel, joins Benhadad of Damascus against Shalmaneser II. of Assyria, 33. Date of his reign, 33. Killed at the battle of Ramoth-Gilead, 33, 99. The first year of Ahab synchronizes with the first year of Jehoshaphat, 98. The twenty-second or last year of Ahab's reign synchronizes with the battle of Karkar on the Orontes, 98. His victory over Benhadad at Aphek, 98

AME

Ahasuerus, Achashverosh, Achashures, meaning of the name, 62. Extent of his dominions, 62
Ahaz, King of Judah, date of, 41. Contemporary with Tiglat Pilesar, 41. Attacked by Pokah of Israel, by Rezin of Damascus, and by the Philistines and Edomites, 41. Joins Tiglat Pilesar at Damascus, which city was captured by the Assyrians, 41. Introduces a sun-dial as an Assyrian innovation, 43, 44. Introduces an altar from Damascus, 43. And introduces also perhaps the astronomical symbolism of the Assyrians, 43, 44. Contemporary with Tiglat Pilesar IV., and with Pekah of Israel, 44
Ahmes, name of, 14
— King of Thebes, 14. Accession, 56
— Admiral, his services under King Ahmes, 16. Drives the foreign rulers out of Avaris, 15. Date of, shown by an inscription, 15
Akkadians, subjugation of the, 18. Language of the highlanders, 20
Anasis of Ptolemy's chronology, 15
Amaziah, reigns with his son Azariah, then sixteen years old, 97
Amenemha I., his name of Arnimos, 101 note. Reforms the Egyptian kalendar in his twenty-first year, when he associated his son Osortesen I. with him in the kingdom, 101 note
Amenemheb, stela of, discovered by Dr. Ebers, 104. The text of this historical document with a complete German translation, 104 note
Amenophis I., the name of the Pharaoh of the exodus, 15. His son Sethos, 15. Length of his reign, 25, 26, 56. Succeeds in recapturing Avaris, and pursues his enemies beyond the Syrian border, 25. Date of his death according to Orosius, 25. The exodus of

AME

the Israelites from Egypt in the reign of, 28. Co-regent with Ahmes, 56
Amonophis II., Pharaoh of Egypt, years of his reign, 57. Exploits of, synchronize with the rule of the Moabites over the Israelites, 58
Ammonites, foreign rulers in Israel, their dominion over the Israelites contemporaneous with the advances of the Pharaohs through Canaan into Mesopotamia, 86
Ammu, the Assyrian name of the sun, 20
Amosis (Amasis), reign of, 60
Ancyra, in Galatia, tablet of, 67, 68
Anianus, the contemporary and editor of the work of Panodorus, 103 *note*
Antediluvian tradition, possible, of 8225 years, 8
Antioch, the church of, founded jointly by St. Peter and St. Paul, 82
Antipas, his marriage with Herodias, 72 *note*. Their separation, 72 *note*
Antipater, son of Herod, execution of, 66
Apamea, Roman census taken in the Syrian city of, 69
Aparanadius, date of the reign of, 32
Apepi, or Apophis, the last of the Hyksos kings, reign of, 14
Aphek, Ahab's victory over Benhadad at, 98
Apis inscription, an, 60
Apocalypse, future fall of Babylon described in the, 6
Apocrypha, knowledge of Jesus of the writings of the, which were forbidden in Palestine, 78. See Genúsim
Apollo Smintheus represented with a mouse in his hand, 52 *note*
Apology, date of the composition of the first, 73
Apostles, the, kept more or less in strict confinement, during the reign of Herod Agrippa I., 79. Exceptionally spared during the general persecution of the Christians, 79. Suddenly led out of prison by an angel, 79
Apostolic council, date of the, 82
Aquila meets with St. Paul at Corinth, 82
Arabian or Canaanite dynasty in Babylon, 19. Possibly identical with Hyksos, the Meles of Beroons, 19-24. Date of the rule of the, in Babylon, 22, 37, 38
Aramæan cities compelled to pay tribute to the Assyrians, 35
Archelaus succeeds Herod, and slays 3000 Jews and Samaritans opposed to his government, 70
Aristotle receives information as to the

ASS

astronomical calculations of the Chaldæans from his relative Callisthenes, 46
Arivarvi of the north, of the Hindu Cush, 17
Arkaianos, date of the reign of, 32. The Arkainanos of the Ptolemæan Canon, Sargon rules in Babylon as, 43
Armais, reign of, 105 *note*
Arnimos, imbessextile kalendar of the first Sothiac period, that of, 100
Arnimos, the name of Amonemha I., and not known to have been borne by any other Pharaoh save Seti I., 101 *note*
'Arpad,' Assyrian 'expedition to,' or to Syria, 34. Date of the Assyrian campaign, 39
Arphaxad, date of, 2
Aryana-Vaëjo, or Aryan home, of the recorded first descendants of Adam, 17
Aryan, or Japhetic, race, traditional sojourn of the, on the highland of Pamer, 10. Indian Aryans, or Japhetites, their rule over Non-Aryans, or Hamites, 18. Separation of the Aryans, which led to the conquest of India, 23
Artaioi, the name of the ancestors of the Persians, 61
Artaxerxes, meaning of the name, 61. Translation of the name by Herodotus, 61
Asarhaddon, contemporary with Mannasseh, 44
Asaridanus, date of the reign of, 32
Ashdod, Sargon makes an expedition to, and to Judah, 42, 43, 59. Date of the expedition, 42
Ashur 'went forth and built Nineveh,' 24. And other cities, 47
Asmonean throne set up by Judas Maccabæus, 66
Aspadas called Astyages by the Greeks, 109
Assyrians, their name of the city of Shinar, 18. Ethnically connected with the Medes and Hyksos, 23
— the book of Genesis on the passage that Ashur 'went forth and built Nineveh,' 23. Probable independence of some of the Assyrians in Mesopotamia, 23. Made tributary by Chedorlaomer, 23. The first Hyksos king in Avaris afraid of the growing power of the Assyrians, 24. Assyrian rule made to synchronize with Hyksos rule, 24. The Ashur of

ASS

Genesis assumed to mean the Assyrians, 24. Their political importance on the expulsion of the Medes from Babylon, 25. The Assyrian annals, and official lists of names, 32. Points of contact hitherto discovered between the Assyrian annals, 32. The 'Canon of Ptolemy' and the Assyrian annals, with the names and dates of the kings, 32. Assyrian and Hebrew synchronisms, 33–44. Harmony between the Hebrew and Assyrian records, 34. 'Disturbance in the city of Assur,' 34. Compel Menahem to pay them tribute, 35. Customary time allowed for the collection of tribute, 35. Date of the first and second Assyrian dynasty, 36. Date of their first conquest of Babylon, 36. Their annals, 36 The first Assyrian dynasty, 36. The second dynasty, 37, 38. The first year of Nabopalassar, 37. The Arabian dynasty of Berosus in Babylon, 37. List of Assyrian and Hebrew synchronisms, 44. Date of the second historical dynasty from Urukh to Darius Codomannus, 46. Origin of Babylonian and Assyrian power, 46. Sargon's inscription that 350 kings had preceded him, 48. The myth about the mice gnawing the bow-strings and shield-thongs of the Assyrians, 51. Harmony established between the Assyrian dates and Hebrew chronology, 87

Assuradinsum, date of the reign of, 32

Assurnahiddin, date of the reign of, 32

Astyages, confusion in the Greek accounts about, 59 note

Atossa, the queen-mother of Xerxes in the 'Persians' of Æschylus, 62

Augustus, Emperor, his census taken in B.C. 3–2, 66. His decree respecting taxation, 67. The censuses of Roman citizens taken by order of, 66, 67. Has an epitome of his public acts drawn up on bronze tablets at Rome, 67

Avaris reoccupied by the Israelites after the Hyksos were expelled, 25. *See* Tanis

Azariah, or Uzziah of Judah, synchronism between him and Tiglat Pilesar, 40. This king contemporary with Pul, king of Assyria, 40, 44

Azi-dahâka, confusion about the, mythical with an historical Daiuccu, 59 note, 109

BAR

BAALTI, the name of, 62
Babel, the builder of the tower of, 37. The 'house of Bel' at, 37. Biblical accounts of the, 47 note
Babylon, future fall of, spoken of by Zechariah, and fully described in the Apocalypse, 6. Capture of, by the Medes (Iranians) in 2458, 9, 16, 18, 83. Commencement of the fourth dynasty in, 12. Date of the expulsion of the Medes by Urukh, 19. Under the rule of Merodach Baladan, 21. Date of the rule of the Arabians in, 22. Taken by the Medes, as given in Genesis, 22. A new king and a new dynasty came to the throne in, B.C. 763, 36. Hopes from further excavations in, 36. The Babylonian annals, 36. Date of the first Assyrian conquest of, 36. Proposed alliance between it and Judah and Egypt, 43. Table of the Babylonian dynasties as restored by us, 45. Origin of Babylonian and Assyrian power, 46. Capture of Nimrod's Babylon, and date of the event, 47. Connection or identification of Nimrod with Merodach, 47. But was possibly peopled by the Chutami of Nabathæan tradition, 48. Babylon in possession of the Japhetic Medes from 2458 to 2234, when Urukh established his rule there, 48. Babylon not the most ancient city in Lower Mesopotamia, 48. Rule of Haman at, 65
Babylonia, first historical inhabitants of, 16. Language of the upper classes and priests of the ancient people of, 20. Japhetites constitute the first historical nation on the Euphrates, the Babylonians, 22
Babylonian, or Assyrian, chronological tradition known probably to Ezra, 9
Babylonians, subjugation of the, 18. Their ancestors ethnically connected with the Abrahamitic Hebrews, 24. The Assyrian divinity Jahu, Jah, Jehovah, 24. Sequence of historical dates preserved by the, 83
Bagoses, general of the Persian army in Samaria, quarrel caused by, 64. His nominee Joshua killed by his brother, 64. Probably kept his promise to Joshua, and helped to procure for him the priesthood, 116. Captures Jerusalem, 116. Imposes a tribute on the Jews, 116. The date of his capture, 117
Baptism, by St. John, in all the country about Jordan, 72. Jesus baptized, 72
Barak, interval between, and the death

BAR

of Ehud, 28. Undetermined period of the victory of, from Ehud to, 86. Barnabas, his journey with St. Paul to Judæa, 82. Charged with St. Paul, by the disciples of Antioch, to convey the collections to relieve the Jews suffering by the famine, 82

Belétaras, King of Assyria, probably a leading general, who succeeded Pul in 745, 40

Beloûs, or Pul, tradition respecting him, transmitted by Alexander Polyhistor, 40

'Bel, house of,' at Babel, 37

Bel-ibni, date of the reign of, 32

Belibus, date of the reign of, 32

Benhadad, of Damascus, his war with Shalmaneser II. of Assyria, 33

Berechaiah, his son Zechariah, 114. Assumed to be stranger in Israel, 115

Berosus, his transmission of Babylonian dates reaching up to 2458, 9. His earliest historical date known to us, namely, the capture of Babylon by the 'Medes,' in 2458, 9. Date of the first and second Assyrian dynasty, 36. Alexander Polyhistor had access to the writings of, 40. Table of the Babylonian dynasties, as restored by us, 45. His statement that in 2458 Babylon existed, and was captured by strangers whom he calls Medes, 48

Bethlehem, murder of the innocents at, 73

Bible, obscurity of the, either by accident or purposely, and known only to the initiated, 31. Completed and corrected by St. Paul and Josephus, 31. Justin Martyr directly refers to a concealment in the Bible, 31. Few chronological errors to be found in it, 31

Biblical development in the Old and New Testament, verbal tradition shown to have been the cause of, 76 *note*

Birch, Dr., the author's indebtedness to him, 41 *note*. His discovery of a previously unknown sign in a name, 101 *note*

Bit-Daiucu, campaign of Sargon against, 109

Bokhoris (Hawk-Horus), the name and title of, given to the last Pharaoh by Orosius, 25 *note*. The King of Egypt, of the twenty-fourth dynasty, first year of, 54. Length of the rule of the twenty-fourth dynasty of, 59, 60. Reigns of Bokhoris I. and II., 60. Bokhoris II. burned alive by Sevek I., 60

CHU

Borsippa, Urukh's tower of 'the seven lights of the earth' at, 47. Meaning of the name, 48 *note*

Bosanquet, his calculations as to the first year of Herod, 66

CAINAN, date of, 2. Possible historical period represented by, 92

Callisthenes, his statement respecting the astronomical calculations of the Chaldæans confirmed, 46. Accompanies Alexander the Great to Asia, and communicates this statement to Aristotle, his relative and teacher, 46

Canaan, date of the conquest of, 21

Carthage, date of the foundation of, 29 *note*

Censorinus, his statement as to the date of the Noachian flood, 11

Chaldæan dynasty, commencement of the second, with Chedorlaomer, 9.

Chaldæan Chronology, connection between Hebrew and, 9

Chaldæans (Chaldi or Celts?), 19. Babylonians as well as Madai, or Medes, of Genesis, 20. Come from the East to Shinar, 23

Champollion, the elder, his two keydates, 104

Chedorlaomer commences' the second Chaldæan dynasty, 9. Defeated by Abraham and his men, in the vale of Shiddim, 12. Probable origin of the name of, 12. His probable object, 18. Probable reason why he made the Assyrians tributary, 23. As King of Elam, 83, 84

Chosroës, King of the Persians, Simplicius flees to, 46

Christ, 'the spiritual Rock,' is the Anointing Spirit or Word of God, 3 *note*, 90, 91

Christian era, commencement of the, 71. The Christian era as at first fixed by Victorinus, or Victorius, of Aquitania, 72

Christians, rising of the, during the reign of Herod Agrippa I., 77 *note*. General persecution of the, during the reign of Herod Agrippa I., 79. Those persecutions put an end to by Herod Agrippa II., 79

Chronology, historical, of the Hebrews, before the time of Solomon, 1. Our results and their indirect bearing on prehistoric times, 88

Chusan Risathaim, a foreign ruler in Israel, reign of, 57. Reign of, over the Israelites, synchronizes with the

CHU

Asiatic campaign of Tuthmoses III. and the policy of his predecessors, 58
Chutami of Nabathæan tradition, were they in Babylon before the time of Nimrod? 48
Cicero, on the date of the foundation of Carthage, 29
Claudius, Emperor, set up by the soldiers by force, 81. Philo's Apology read before the senate in this reign, 81
Clement of Alexandria, his date of the birth of Jesus, 66. His errors, 66, 67
Colchians were Cushites or non-Aryans, 24
Constantine, the New Testament not finally revised before the time of, 71
Cooper, Mr. Basil H., the author's indebtedness to him, 41 note. On the reign of Osorkon I., 54. On the accession of Tuthmoses III., 56. On the date of the accession of Thothmes the Great, 99. On Shishak I. and Psusennes II. co-regents, 106
Cossaei, the, of classical writers, 47
'Cross among all nations, the symbol of the,' a forthcoming work, 89 note. The Cross the symbol of Divine enlightenment, 91
Crucifixion of Jesus, date of the, 74-78
Ctesias, his testimony probably underrated, 2. His dates for the foundation of Assyrian power, 24. His birth at Cnidus in Caria, 49. The companion of Artaxerxes Mnemon, 49. His history of Persia, and his knowledge of cuneiform inscriptions, 49. Leaves Persia, 49. His account of Assyrian kings from the foundation of Nineveh to Pul, 49. States that Aspadas was called Astyages by the Greeks, 109
Cuneiform inscriptions, knowledge of Ctesias of, 49. Their chronological accuracy, 49. The Assyrian annals confirmed, 87
Cush, the land of, 21, 17. Locality of the, 17
Cushites, the Colchians were, or non-Aryans, 24. Nimrod called in Genesis 'the son of Cush,' 47. The land of Cush, adjoining the Eden of Genesis, and watered by the Gihon, 17. The inscription respecting 'the heretic race of Kesh,' and their dwelling-place, 17
Cyaxares, or Dejoces, revolt of the Medes under, 59
Cyrus, the anointed of God, gives permission to the Israelites to return from Babylon to Judæa, 5, 63

EDO

DAIUCCU of cuneiform inscriptions, 59 note. Transported to Hamath, 59 note, 108. Exploits of a mythical Azi-da-haka with, 109. Probably recovers and extends his dominions, 109. The name in Assyrian, 110
Dalta or Rita, chief of Ellibi, 109
Damascus, an altar from, introduced by Ahaz into Judah, 43. Attacked and taken by Tiglat Pilesar, 41. Conquered by Abraham, who ruled there shortly after he left Haran, 84
Daniel, Book of, on the division of the Persian empire into Satrapies, 62
Darius, origin of the name, 61. Possible origin of the legend about the horse of, 62 note
— Codomannus, date of, 46
— Hystaspes, date of the reign of, 4. Hystaspes-Vashtaspa, the name of, 62. The real founder of the Persian monarchy, 62. His name in the book of Esther, 62. Renews the edict of Cyrus, 63. Loses his influence in Europe after the battle of Marathon, and probably in Syria also, 66
David, King, ethnical connections of the Rechabites with, 25. Years of his reign, 86
Deiokes, confusion in the Greek accounts about, 59 note
— and Daiuccu, Mr. Sayce's remarks on, 108. The name Deiokes possible among the Medes in the eighth century B.C., 109
Dejoces, whom Diodorus calls Cyaxares, revolt of the Medes under, 59
Deluge, Noachian, lists of patriarchs before and after the, 2. Its date after Censorinus, 11. Must not be literally, but figuratively, interpreted, 17
Dido of the Phœnicians, the Elissa of Virgil, 62 note
Dionysian era, 71, 72
Dionysius Exiguus, his era began with the birth of Jesus, 72

EBER, date of, 2
Ebers, Dr., stela of Amenemheb, edited by, 104 note
Ecclesiasticus, the ancient and probably the original title of, 112
Eclipse, solar, in the year 763, 36
Eden of second chapter of Genesis, 17
Edomites attack Ahaz of Judah, who is succoured by Tiglat Pilesar, to whom Ahaz pays tribute, 41

EGY

Egypt, proposed alliance between it and Babylon and Judah, 43. The twelfth dynasty and Hyksos, 48–60, Shishak's capture of Jerusalem, 50. Synchronisms between the history of Egypt and of other countries, 50. Advance of Tirhaka of Ethiopia into Egypt, where Tirhaka slew Sevek, or Sabako, 51. Tirhaka sues for peace, according to an inscription of Sargon, 51. The Egyptian tradition mentioned to Herodotus omitted Tirhaka and Sabako, 51. The myth about the mice gnawing the bow-strings and shield-thongs of the Assyrians, 51. Political treaty between the rivals of the twenty-first and twenty-second dynasties, 54. The twenty-second dynasty not superseded by the twenty-third, but continued to reign contemporaneously with it, 54. Number of years which Eusebius gives for the reign of the nineteenth dynasty, 55. Years assigned by Manetho to the twenty-first and twenty-second dynasties, 55. Date of the accession of the eighteenth dynasty, 56. Nebuchadnezzar's real or expected conquest of Egypt, to which the Book of Ezekiel refers, 60. The exodus from, 84. Date of the exodus, 85. The Tanite co-regent, 107. Memory of earlier foreign conquest blotted out by the horrors of Omar and his hordes, 103

Egyptians, Japhetites constitute the aboriginal Egyptian (not African) nation, 22. Their first attack of the Hebrews in Egypt, 26. Their enemies the Sharutana and the Tsakruri, 57. Make an alliance with the Philistines and the Sharutana, 58. The era of the battle of Actium, 66. Harmony of the Manethonian dates with the monuments, 87. The lunar feriæ of the, referred to, 104. Like the modern Jews, they reckoned two new moon feriæ in each lunar month, 105. Value of these lunar feriæ as notes of time, 105. The lunar cyclo of the imbissextile, or vague, Egyptian kalendar of exactly 365 days, 105

Ehud, death of, 28. The undetermined period from the death of, to Barak's victory, 86

El, the Babylonian divinity, regarded as identical with the El, Eljon, and Elohim of the Abrahamitic Hebrews, 24. Identity of the Babylonian divinity El with the Assyrian divinity

EUS

Jahu, and with the El and Jah-Jehova of the Hebrews, 25 note

Elam, a Cushite population in, in the pre-historic times of Nimrod, 47

Eleazar, line of Aaronites called after, 110. The line of, twice mentioned in the Chronicles, 111

Elephantine festival tablet, 100

Eliashib, death of, 65

Elissa, Virgil's, the Dido of the Phœnicians, 62 note

Eljon (El-On), the name, 25 note

Eilat-Gula, Queen of Babylon, date of the reign of, 20. Of the house of Sargon I., 37. Followed by Hammurabi, 37

Ellibi supposed to have been Ekbatana, 109. Campaign of Sargon against, 109. Probable cause of Sargon's interference, 109. Ipsabara placed on the throne by Sargon in preference to his brother Nibe after the death of their father Dalta, or Rita, 109

Elohistic part of the Mosaic writings referring to Indian (Babylonian) tradition, 25 note

Elulæus, King of Babylon, date of the reign of, 32

Enoch, date of, 2. Possible historical period represented by, 92

Enos, date of, 2. Contemporary with Seth, 4. Period of, suggested, 9, 91

Ephah, removal of the, to the land of Shinar to build a house unto the wickedness, 63

Ephesus, St. Paul's stay of two years at, 82

Eponyms, Assyrian, 32

Era, Dionysian, 71, 72. Of the battle of Actium, 66

Esther, Book of, the name of the king mentioned in the, 62. Esther or Hadassah is clearly the same name as Atossa, the queen-mother of Xerxes in the 'Persians' of Æschylus, 62. She brings about the destruction of Haman, 65. Her part in the palace intrigue, which put Mordechai in the place of Haman, 117

Ethiopians, the twenty-fifth dynasty of, date of their reign, in Egypt, 59, 60

Euphrates, called also the Gihon, 47

Eusebius on Pul, King of Assyria, 33. Number of years which he gives for the reign of the nineteenth dynasty, 55. The Armenian version of his Chronicle, 81. Transmits and confirms the tradition as to the foundation of the church in Rome, 81, 82

INDEX.   125

EXO

Exodus of Abraham from Haran, period of the, 9, 11, 13, 18, 84, 85
Exodus of the Hebrews from Egypt, date of the, 14
— period of, to the foundation of the Temple, 8, 85. Name of the Pharaoh of the exodus, 15. Assumed date of, 15. Date of the exodus of the Israelites from Egypt, according to Hebrew chronology, 20. Reign and death of the Pharaoh of the, 26. Positive biblical date for the event, 27, 29. Implied Hebrew date for it, 27. Incorrectness of the date in the second Book of Kings between the exodus and the foundation of the Temple, 27. Period from the exodus to the foundation or dedication of the Temple, 85.
Ezekiel, the Divine command in the Book of, that the sons of Zadok only should stand before God, 111. The fact acknowledged and condemned that Israel has brought into the sanctuary strangers uncircumcised in the heart and uncircumcised in the flesh, 111, 112
Ezra, scheme of Hebrew chronology before the time of, 4. Knowledge of the initiated contemporaries of Ezra, of the millennium, 6. The unhistorical and unprophetic scheme of, 6. Date of Ezra's mission to Jerusalem, and assumed to be sanction, if not suggest, the scheme which has given rise to the theory of the millennium, 7. May have known of a Babylonian or Assyrian chronological tradition, 9. His mission to Jerusalem, and the date of it, 62. Appointed governor, 62. Date of his governorship with power over life and death, 63. Ezra and the Purim, 63. Dissatisfied Jews obtained permission from the Persian king to be allowed to build a temple at Gerizim, 63. His public reading of the law, 63. Great synagogue under, 63. His despotic measures, 64. End of his governorship, if not of his life, 65, 117

FLOOD stories more or less similar to that of Genesis, and their antiquity, 17. See Noachian deluge
— Samaritan, the year of the, 10
Foreign rulers in Israel, 57

GADITES led into captivity by Tiglat Pileser, 33
Gaius meets with St. Paul at Corinth, 82
Galilee, Jesus began to preach in, 73

HEB

Genesis, necessary ethnic interpretation of what in Genesis is called the birth of Shem, 17. Havilah or Chavilah referred to in, 18.
Gentísim or Apocrypha, origin and authority of, 113.
Gerizim, temple of, built, 63
Ghost, Holy, 'the rock' a symbolical expression for the, 3 note
Gihon-Oxus, the banks of the, the recorded dwelling-place of the first descendants of Adam, 17
Gihon, the river, 17. The Euphrates and the Nile also so called, 47
Gospel, preaching of the, to the poor and uninitiated, 89

HALIBURTON, R. G., of Nova Scotia, his discovery of the connection of the Pleiades with mythology and the calendars, 8 note
Haman, his rule at Babylon, 65. His enmity to the Jews, 65. The influence of the 'Stranger in Israel' increased by Haman, 65. Desirability of upsetting Haman in Babylon, 65. Which was effected by Esther, the Benjamite, 65. Mordechai set up in Haman's place, 65
Hamath, expedition to, 34
Hamites (Aryans and Turyans?), their original dwelling-place, 16. Assumed combination of Hamites and Japhetites, in Mesopotamia, 17. Subjugation of the, 18. Ruled over by Japhetites, and become their servants or slaves, long before the time of Noah, 18. Ruled by Japhetites, and follow their Indian brethren to Mesopotamia, 23
Hammurabi, the deity of, 21. Cylinder of, and the events recorded by it, 37. The first king of a foreign race, and follows Queen Ellat-Gula of the house of Sargon I., 37. Date of his reign, 38
Hanani comes to Nehemiah with a complaint about the destruction of the walls and gates of Jerusalem, 64
Haran, period of the exodus of Abraham from, 9. Date of, 11, 13, 85. His exodus and its causes, 18
Hasael, his war with Shalmaneser II., 33
Havilah, or Chavilah, referred to, in Genesis, 18
Hebrews, historical chronology of the, before the time of Solomon, question of, 1. Scheme of Hebrew chronology before the time of Ezra, 4. Haliburton's discovery of the twenty-three Pleiades periods of seventy-two

years, 8. Connection between Hebrew and Chaldæan chronology, 9. Commencement of Hebrew chronology, shown by the Median capture of Babylonia in 2458 B.C., 10. Hebrew tradition goes back to the time of Eden, 10. The servitude of the Hebrews in Mesopotamia and Egypt, 12, 13. Called 'the lepers,' 16. Their exodus from Egypt, 16. Their ethnic relations, 16. Meaning of their name, 16. First settlements of, in Mesopotamia, 16. Date of the advance of the Israelites under Joshua from Shiddim, 21. Regarded as Indians from the East to Shinar, where Iranian Medes joined them, 24. Identity of the Babylonian divinity El with the Assyrian divinity Jahu, and with the Hebrew El and Jah-Jehova, 25 note. Exodus of the Israelites from Egypt in the reign of Amenophis, 26. Reach the Red Sea before Amenophis was informed of it, 26. Entry of the Hebrews into Avaris, 26. The Israelites the lepers of Manetho, 26. Contemporary reigns of kings of Israel with kings of Assyria, Babylonia, and Egypt, 33-44. Sufferings of the Jews by famine, 82. Sequence of historical dates preserved by the, 83. Their ancestors had lived in Ur of the Chaldees, 83. Table of Hebrew chronology from the death of Solomon to the destruction of the Temple, 93. Biblical authorities for the length of the reigns in Judah and Israel, 97. Following running numbers in our table of Hebrew regnal years, 99, 100.

Hebron-Kirjath-Arba, date of the building of, 13, 14. Date of Abraham's residence in, 13

Herod, year of the death of, 66. Death of, 69, 70

— Agrippa I., persecution of the Christians under, 77 note. His Asmonean (Sadducean?) descent, 79. His martyrdom of St. Stephen, 79. Beheads St. James, 79. His rule of terror, which lasted three years, 79. Throws St. Peter into prison, from which he escapes marvellously, 79

— Agrippa II., puts an end to the persecutions of the Christians, 79

Herodias, her marriage with Antipas, 72 note. Their separation, 72 note

Herodotus, the Assyrians called Arabians by, 21. On the Medes as Aryans, but they afterwards change

their name, 24. On the division of the Persian empire into Satrapies, 62 Hezekiah (the Hazakiahu of inscriptions), contemporary of Sargon during the last seventeen years of his reign, and during the first eight years of Sennacherib, 41. Jerusalem besieged by Sargon, and a tribute imposed on Hezekiah, 43. This tribute enforced by Sennacherib ten years later, 43. Years of his reign, and of kings of Assyria, 44. Advance of Tirhakah, King of Ethiopia, accompanied by pestilence, 44. Date of his illness and recovery, 52. His ally Yavani given up to Sargon, 52. Sends an ambassador to the Assyrians with tribute, 35. This tribute imposed not at Lakish but at Jerusalem, 35. His 'precious molten metal' taken to Nineveh, 35.

Hilkiah, the high priest and contemporary of Jeremiah, if his father, 114. A priest of Anatoth, 114. Promised the Rechabites an eternal priesthood, 114

Himalaya, residence of the Medo-Iranians in, before the conquest of India, 23 Hincks, Dr., identifies Men-peh-Ra with Theon's Menophres, 102

Hiram, King of Tyre, date of, 29

Horus, date of the reign of, 56. Years of his reign, 57

Hosea, date of the reign of, 42. Tiglat Pilesar claims to have set up, but probably only confirmed him, 42. Contemporary with Shalmaneser IV., for five years, 42. Made prisoner by Sargon, 42

Hammurabi, King of Babylon, date of the reign of, 20. King or chief of the Cassi (Cossaei), 20. His name connected with the Assyrian Ammu, the sun, 20

Hyksos, the first of the race of the, 11. Their national god Seth, and their temple to him at Tanis-Avaris, 11. Origin of the name, 14. The regency of Joseph under a Hyksos-Pharaoh, 15. And why this Pharaoh knew not Joseph, 14. Driven out from Tanis-Avaris, 16. Pharaoh kindly received Abraham the Hebrew, 13. Reason for alliance with Hebrews, 13. The symbol of the serpent among the, 12. Their possible ethnic relations with the Medes of Berosus, and the Arabian rulers of Babylon, 12. Whence came the hosts of the Hyksos, and what became of them? 19. Object of

INDEX. 127

Chodorlaomer to drive them from Egypt, 19. Number of years spent by them in Egypt, 20. Date of the Hyksos-rule in Egypt, 22. Their features on the monuments, 21, 22. Belong to some specific tribes of their Medo-Iranian brethren, 23. And would welcome Abraham to Egypt, 23. Ethnically connected with the Assyrians proper, 23. The Hyksos rule made to synchronize with Assyrian rule, 24. Ethnically the same as the Arabians or Medes, and connected with them as Iranians, 24. Recalled by the Israelites from Jerusalem to Avaris, and from thence ruled thirteen more years over Egypt, 25. Their final expulsion from Avaris and Egypt, 26. Date of the second Hyksos rule of thirteen years, according to Manetho, 56. Expulsion of the Hyksos, 56. A Manethonian total from their expulsion by Amasis to the end of Dyn. XIX., 103. Part they took with the Hebrews in the battle of Shiddim, 84. Date of the final expulsion of the, 85, 101
Hystaspes, Vashtaspa, Bactrian king of the Iranians, probably an ancestor of Sargon II., 10 note. See Darius

IL-YA, 'my God,' the name, 25 note
India, conquest of, referred to in Genesis as Havilah or Chavilah, 18. Aryan separation which led to the conquest of, 23
Indians, subjugation of the Indians, 18
Iranians, the Hyksos, Arabians, and Medes ethnically connected as, 24. The Iranian was the stranger in Israel, 24. Reference in the Mosaic writings to the Jehovistic part of the Assyrian or Iranian tradition, 25 note
Irenæus on the age of Jesus, 73. Passage in the fourth Gospel by, 76. Connection of this Gospel with the beloved disciple, and with the first three Gospels, 76
Isaac, date of, 2
Ischita and religious reformer of the Nabathæans, 9 note
Ishita-Seth-Zoroaster, the first king of the Median dynasty of Babylon, may have received the name of Zoroaster, 9, 10 note
Israel, the Iranian, 'the stranger in,' 24, 25 note, 109. List of foreign rulers in, 56. And list of contemporary reigns of Pharaohs, 57. Two lines of Aaronites in, 110

Israelites, Jeremiah's prophecy of the seventy years of exile of the, 4. Cyrus gives permission to the Israelites to return to Judæa, 5. Had no dealings with the Egyptians after the exodus, but were dangerous foes, 58. Necessity for the dominion of the nations of Palestine for the Egyptians, 58
Ithamar, line of Aaronites called after, 110. The second priesthood of the stranger connected with the Aaronic line of Ithamar, 111. Omitted in the Chronicles, 111
Ituræans, war made by the Romans against them, 69

JACOB, date of, 2. Receives a tradition from Shem, and transmits it to the mother of Moses, 3
Jahu, Jah, Jehovah, the Assyrian divinity, first proclaimed by Moses among the Hebrews, 25. Mr. Sayce thinks that Jahu must be given up, 25 note. Ilubihd is substituted for Jahubihd, 25 note
Jahu, Jah, Jehova, the name of, received through the Hebrews, as the only representatives of pure Monotheism, 24 note. The proclamation of Jehovah referred in Genesis to the days of Seth, 24 note. Difference between the Jehovistic and Elohistic traditions, 25 note
James, St., his martyrdom, 79. Trusted by Sadducees, 79
Jao, 25 note
Japhetites, the first historical inhabitants of Shinar, 16. Assumed combination of Japhetites and Hamites in Mesopotamia, 17. As Indian Aryans, their rule over Non-Aryans, or Hamites, 18. 'Japhet shall dwell in the tents of Shem,' that is, in Mesopotamia, 18. Rule Ham in Mesopotamia, 22. Constitute the aboriginal Egyptian (not African) nation, as well as the first historical nation on the Euphrates, the Babylonians, 22. Abraham regarded as an Aryan or Japhetite chief, 23. Settle in the east in Shinar-Babylonia, 23
Jared, date of, 2. Possible historical period represented by, 92
Jehoshaphat, regency of, 33. The first year of, synchronizes with the first year of Ahab, 98
Jehova, the Jahu of the Assyrians or Iranians, 'men began to publish the name of,' 9 note

JEH

Jehovah-Zabaot, the name of, and the promise of Jeremiah, 110
Jehovistic part of the Old Testament, the Jehovistic 'strangers' the Rechabites, ethnically connected with David, Jethro, and Melchizedek, 25 *note*. Mosaic writings referring to Iranian (Assyrian) tradition, 25 *note*
Jehozadak, father of the high priest Joshua, 113
Jehu, his war with Shalmaneser II., 33. Contemporary with Shalmaneser II, of Assyria, 44
Jephtha, length of time from his judgeship to the division of the land under Joshua, 29, 86
Jeremiah, his prophecy of the seventy years of exile of the Israelites, 4. The seventy periods of, enlarged to seventy jubilee periods, 5. The seventy years of his prophecy, 61. His promise in the name of Jehovah-Zabaot, 110. His promise to the sons of Jonadab, 111
Jeroboam, his flight into Egypt unto King Shishak, and was in Egypt until the death of Solomon, 27, 55
— II. reigns with his son Zachariah, 28
Jerome, St., transmits and confirms the tradition of the foundation of the Church in Rome, 81, 82
Jerusalem, captured by the Egyptians under their king Shishak 1., 49, 55. Tribute imposed by the Assyrians on the Jews not at Lakish, but at Jerusalem, 35. Besieged, and a tribute imposed by Sargon, 43. This tribute enforced by Sennacherib ten years later; 43. Complaint of Hanani to Nehemiah about the broken walls, 64. Bagoses enters the city, and forces his way into the Temple, 64. Punishes the Jews during seven years, 64. Probably leaves an army to enforce the tribute from them, 64. Nehemiah sent as governor to Jerusalem, 65. The destruction of the city made to coincide with the mystic year 70, dated from the supposed nativity of Jesus, 72
Jesus, years of the birth and death of, 66-78. His genealogy and the parts into which it is divided, 71. Information given by Clement of Alexandria, 66. Events which caused the journey of Joseph and Mary from Galilee to Bethlehem, 69. Birth of Jesus, 69, 70 *note* 71. The statement of St. Luke that Jesus was thirty when he

JOH

began to teach, 72. Attention shown to have been directed early in the second if not in the first century to the date of the birth of Jesus, 72. Baptized by John, 72. Began to preach in Galilee, 73. Age when he began to preach, 73. Justin Martyr's statement as to his birth, 73. Irenæus on the age of Jesus, 73. The recorded murder of the children at Bethlehem, 73. Date of the crucifixion, 74-78. The temple of his body, 75. His age in the first year of his ministry, 76. Saying of the Jews to him, 76. His age according to St. Matthew when he went with his parents to Jerusalem, 77 *note*, 78. Had probably more followers in Samaria than in Judæa, and was called by the Jews 'a Samaritan,' 77 *note*. Explanation of his general reference to the Septungint version, 78. His knowledge of the writings of the Apocrypha, which were forbidden in Palestine, 78. His stay in Egypt about 10, his age 48 years, 78
Jesus or Joshua, the son of Sirach of Jerusalem, 113. His collection of the grave and short sentences of wise men that had gone before him, 113. The Hebrew original of this known to St. Jerome, 113. Remark of Athanasius respecting it, 113. Called in the Talmud 'the son of Eleazar,' 113
Jethro, ethnical connections of the Rechabites with, 25
— one of the Kenites, 110. Priesthood of, 111
Jews, 3000 of them slain by Archelaus for their opposition to his government, 70
Jochebed, mother of Moses, transmits the 'holy' tradition to Moses, 3
Johannan, high priest of the Temple at Jerusalem, quarrels with his brother Joshua, whom he slays in the Temple, 64. Connected with the high priest Joshua and his adversary, 112. Murders his brother, the high priest Joshua, 110, 112.
John, St., expects the millennium in his time or soon after, and had no knowledge of the unhistorical and unprophetic scheme of the time of Ezra, 6 His baptism of Jesus, 72. Put into the prison of Machærus, 72 *note*. John put aside as a demagogue, 72 *note*. On the age of Jesus while he was a teacher, 73. The reference

JON

in his Gospel to the age of Jesus, 75
Jonadab, possibly a brother of David, 111. Patriarch and lord of the Rechabites, 111. Jeremiah's promise to the sons of, 111
Joseph, date of, 2. And of his regency, 14. Reason why Pharaoh knew not Joseph, 14. Date of the Pharaoh of Joseph, 14. The title of Zaphnat-Pa'hneach, or 'procurer of life,' given to him by Pharaoh, 14
Josephus, his correction of a date in the second Book of Kings, 27. His statement in detail, 28 and *note*. Indebted to Menander for the Tyrian annals, 29. Passage in his 'Antiquities' referring to the year of Ezra's governorship, 64. His account of a Cyrus whom the Greeks called Artaxerxes, 65. His account of the death of Herod and of his son Antipater, 66, 69, 70. His statement respecting the imprisonment of St. John, 72 *note*. Gives credence to Nicolaus of Damascus, 84. His dates, and the sources of his information, 86. Draws from an unwritten tradition, 89. Gives us a Manethonian total from the expulsion of the Hyksos by Amasis to the end of Dyn. XIX., 56, 103
Joshua, his conquest connected with the friendly rule of Arabians (Hyksos?) in Babylon, 21. Time of his dividing the land, 29. Knowledge of the initiated contemporaries of, of the millennium, 6. His five years before the division of the land, 85
Joshua, the high priest, grandson of Seraja or Sirach, the son of Eleazar or Azariah, the high priest, 63, 113. Foundations of the Temple and of the walls laid under, 63. Promised the high priesthood by the Persian general Bagoses, 64. Quarrel between the two brothers in the Temple, when Joshua is slain by his 'brother,' Johannan, according to Josephus, 64, 110. Perhaps the 109th Psalm refers to Joshua and his adversary, and the 84th to Joshua 'the anointed,' 112. His acts condemned by Ezekiel, but approved of by Jeremiah, 111, 112. Seems to have been the reviser of the 'Proverbs' or 'Wisdom of Sirach,' 112. His father Jehozadak, 113. Possibly composes the 110th Psalm, 114
Judæa, a Persian army of occupation in, 64. Formation of a Judæan camp

LPE

and a Samaritan camp, amongst the Israelites in Judæa, 64, 65. Taxed by the Roman governor, 67. Quirinus appointed governor of, 67. Taxing takes place in, at the time of Herod's death, 69. Sargon's campaign to, 43. Proposed alliance between it and Babylon and Egypt, 43. Sargon's campaign against, which he subdues, 69
Judah, his marriage to Thamar, perhaps a matrimonial metaphor, 109
Judas Maccabeus sets up the Asmonean throne, 66
— of Gamala, his attempted revolt of the people, 68
— of Sephôris, his revolt of the people, 68
Judges, Book of, St. Paul and Josephus on the chronology of the, 28
Judith, Book of, as a possible allegory referring to the days of Purim, 62 *note*
Justin Martyr, his statement as to the age of Jesus, 73

KALDI, or priests in Wales and Iona, 20. The Kaldi first met with on the Persian Gulf, whence they went northward and possessed themselves (under Merodach Baladan) of Babylon, 21
Kaldu of the Ebers, inscription, 20
Kames, King of Thebes, father of Ahmes, mentioned as Tsafento, 14
Karalla, campaign of Sargon against, 109
Karkar, on the Orontes, battle of, 33. Date of the battle, 33. Synchronizes with the twenty-second or last year of Ahab's reign, 98
Karnack festival list, 104 *note*
Kassi, the, in Elam-Babylonia, 21
Kenites, 'strangers in Israel,' 110. Their ethnical connection with the Rechabites, 110
Khsha, Shah, derivation of the word, 62
Kineladanus, date of the reign of, 32
Kinzirus, King of Babylon, date of the reign of, 32
Kudur-Lagamer, probably set up in Babylon, as ruler of Elam and Syria in 1992, when Abraham left Haran; identical with Chedorlaomer, 12, 83, 84
Kudur-Mabuk, ruler of Elam and Syria, King of Sumir and Akkad, co-regent with Elatagula, defeated by Hammurabi, Chron. Tables, col. 1

LAMECH, date of, 2, 3. Possible historical period represented by, 91
Lepsius, his 'Königsbuch' published

LEN

in 1858, 102. His Sothiac date of Thothmes the Great, 103
Lenormant, C., his suggestion, 17 *note*
— His unpublished discovery of Sumiri-tuv, Samir-Asshur, and Sungir (Singara-Sinar), 18 *note*. Proof of the latter derivation, 18 *note*
Levi, 'holy' tradition transmitted by Jacob to, and thus to Moses, 3
Luke, St., his statement respecting the first taxes, 67, 68. Says that Jesus was thirty when he began to teach, 72
Lunar Feria, list of the thirty, referred to, 101

MAHALALEEL, date of, 2. Possible historical period represented by, 92
Maka-Tyra attacked by Ramesses III., 57. Supplied by the sea with fish, 57
Manasseh, half tribe of, led into captivity by Tiglat Pilesar, 33.
— King of Judah, his tribute sent to Nineveh, 35. Contemporary with Asarhaddon, King of Assyria, 44
Manetho, on the Pharaoh of Joseph, 13. His date of the death of (the Pharaoh of the exodus) Amenophis I., 25. On Avaris, twice attacked and once occupied by the lepers (Israelites), 25. A priest of the city of Sebennytus, who lived during the reign of Ptolemy I., 50. His dates, 50, 60. His statement respecting the celebration of the first Olympiad in Egypt during the forty years' reign of Petubastes, 50. His period of 393 years verified, 50. Harmony of the Manethonian dates with the monuments, 56, 87. A forged treatise put forth as a genine work of Manetho, 102. The title of the book 'Sothis,' or 'The Dogstar,' 102. His reign interposed between Mesphra-Tuthmosis (Men-shepor-Ra Thothmes III.) and Menophres Ramses I., 105
Marathon, date of the battle of, 62, 66. Effects of the battle upon Darius Hystaspes and Nehemiah, 66
Mardok Empados, the Merodach Baladan of the Babylonian annals, date of the reign of, 32. Deposed by Sargon, 43
Maruduk, or Morodach, the deity of Hammurabi, King of Cushites, 21
Mary, events which caused her journey from Galilee to Bethlehem, 69
Medes, the Colchian, in Mesopotamia with the Medes, 24

MER

'Medes,' their capture of Babylon in 2458, 9
Medes (Iranians) take Babylon, 16, 18. Their possible ethnic relations with the Hyksos and the Arabians, who ruled in Babylon, 19. Expelled from Babylon, 19. The symbol of the serpent among the, 19. The Madai of Genesis, 20. King of the Medes from the Caspian called Zoroaster, from the great Monotheist, 23. Ethnically connected with the Assyrians proper, 23. Herodotus on the Medes as Aryans and as non-Aryans, 24. Political importance of the Assyrians on the expulsion of the Medes from Babylon, 24. Called the Madai in the Bible, their rule in Babylon, 46. Capture of Babylon by strangers whom Berosus calls Medes, 48. Babylon in their hands from 2458 to 2234, when Urukh expelled them and established his rule there, 48. Years of the rule of the Medes at Nineveh, 49. Their revolt under Dejoces, whom Diodorus calls Cyaxares, 59. Their language and their linguistically related neighbours, 109
Medo-Iranians, their residence in the north of the Himalaya, 23
Megiddo, battle which ended with the taking of, 104
Melchizedek, ethnical connections of the Rechabites with, 25. A type of the Messiah, 111. A priest of the highest God, and yet a non-Hebrew, 111. A priesthood after the order of, 111
Menahem, King of Israel, pays tribute to the King of Assyria, 33. Date of his reign, 34. Compelled by the Assyrians to pay tribute to them, 35. Called Menahem of Samaria in the Assyrian annals, 35, 39. The annals do not refer to the personal presence of Menahem, 39
Menander on the date of Carthage, 29
Menephtha, the divine part of the name of, 102
Menophres of the Era, under whom the astronomer Theon made the second Sothiac period begin with B.C. 1323, 101
— His name involving the Sun-god Ra, 102. His agreement with the Elephantine inscription, 103
— Ramses I., era of, 105. His reign, 106
Merodach, (Nimrod?), the god of Hammurabi, King of Cushites, 21, 47
— Baladan of the Bible becomes King of Babylon, deposed by Sargon,

MER

King of Assyria, 43. His embassy to King Hezekiah, 43, 59. Date of the embassy and its object, 43. The enquiry after the 'wonder which was done in the land,' 43

Meroe, King of, sues Sargon for peace, 59

Mesopotamia, first settlement of the Shemites in, 16, 17. Independent Assyrians at, made tributary to Chedorlaomer, 23

Messianic millennium, the theory of the, 61

Messiah, the promised, a son of David, a non-Hebrew, 111. Melchizedek a type of the, 111

Methuselah, date of, 2. Contemporary with Adam, 2. Transmits the history of Eden, Adam and Eve, and the serpent, to Noah and his sons, 2. His death, according to the Hebrew text, 2. According to the Septuagint, 2. Possible historical period represented by, 22

Mice revered by the people of Troas, 52 *note*. Reason for this, 52 *note*

Midianites, foreign rulers in Israel, reigns of, 57. This period synchronizes with the reign of Ramesses II., 58

Migdol probably not attacked by Ramesses III., 57

Millennium, a type of the future, 5. Knowledge of the initiated contemporaries of Zerubbabel, of Joshua and Ezra, as to the, 6. Table of the second half of the 7,000 years, or from the destruction of the first Temple to the end of the millennium, 6. Future fall of Babylon described in the Apocalypse, 6

Mishna, rule noted in the, respecting the first year of a king's reign, 30

Moabites, foreign rulers in Israel, reigns of, 57. Their rule synchronizes with the exploits of Amenophis II., 58. The dominion of the, over the Israelites contemporaneous with the advances of the Pharaohs through Canaan into Mesopotamia, 86

Mordecai set up in the place of Haman, 65

Moses, date of, 2. First proclaims the (Assyrian?) divinity Jahu, Jah, Jehovah, among the Hebrews, which had not been known to their Hebrew forefathers, 24. Difference in the Mosaic writings between the Jehoristic and Elohistic traditions, 24, 25 *note*. The forty years of Moses from the exodus to his death, 85

NIM

'Mountain of the world,' position of, according to Genesis and Babylonian tradition, 16

Müller, Professor J. G., on the Shemites in their relations to Hamites and Japhetites, 17 *note*

NABATHÆAN tradition, the Chutami of, 48

Nabonadius, the broken cylinder of, and its records, 37

Nabonassar, date of the reign of, 32. Era of, 46

Nabopalassar, eclipse of the moon in the fifth year of, 29. First year of, 37

Nadius, King of Babylon, date of the reign of, 32

Nahor, date of, 2

Nebuchadnezzar, date of his destruction of the Temple, 4. His real or expected conquest of Egypt, to which the Book of Ezekiel refers, 60. Causes the high priest Serajah to be slain at Riblah, 112

Necho. *See* Neku

Nehemiah appointed governor after Ezra, 62. Date of the last year of his rule, 62. Present at the foundation of the Temple and of the walls, 63. Covenant sealed with, and peace and concord established, 63. Complaint of Hanani to him, 64. Sent as governor to Jerusalem, 65. Length of his governorship, 65. His last journey to Jerusalem, 66

Neku (Necho), reign of, 60

Nero, date of the death of, 82

Nicolaus of Damascus, the friend of Herod and Augustus, credence given to, by Josephus, 84

Nile, called also the Gihon, 47

Nile-god, statue of the, dedicated to Prince Shishak, 106, 108. Examined by Dr. Birch and Mr. Cooper, 108

Nimrod, the son of Cush, 21. Establishment of, in the plain, 47. Probably by the Assyrians (Sumir), first called Shinar, connected with the city of Erech, 47. Capture of Nimrod's Babylon by the Medes of Berosus, and the date, 47. Nimrod called in Genesis 'the son of Cush,' 47. A Cushite population in Elam probably already in the prehistoric times of Nimrod, 47. He may have ruled over the Non-Aryans or Cushites (Turyans?), originally from the countries about the Hindu-Cush, 47

NIN

Nineveh, Ashur 'went forth and built,' 24, 47, 49. Dates of Ctesias for the foundation of Assyrian power, 24. The city of Nineveh when built, 24. Hezekiah's 'precious molten metal' taken by the Assyrians to, 35. Date when Ashur went forth from Shinar to build the city with its temple of Ishtar, 49. The city of Nineveh may have existed when Abraham left Haran, and when Chedorlaomer began to reign, 49

Noachian deluge, time required intervening between the Flood and the creation of Adam, 7. Possible antediluvian tradition of 8225 years, 8. Intentional shortening of the pre-Noachian period to 1656 years, 8. The unabbreviated periods of Genesis which precede the record of the Noachian deluge preserved by the channels of tradition, 9. The Hebrew date for the, 10, 11, 83

Noah, date of, 2. The pre-Noachian period unhistorically shortened, made to appear historical, 4. Prophecy of, relating to the Japhetites and Hamites, 18. Possible historical period represented by, 22

OLYMPIAD, the first, celebrated in Egypt, 50. Regnal year of the first Olympiad, 51
Omar and his hordes in Egypt, horrors committed by them, 104
Oppert, Dr., reference to, 46 *note*
Orchamus, or Urchamus. *See* Urukh
Orontes, Assyrian expedition to the, 33, 34
Orosius, the Spanish presbyter, on the date of the death of the Pharaoh of the exodus, 25, 85. Sources of his information, 85
'Osirian,' the Egyptian mortuary epithet, or 'justified,' 108
Osorkon I., year in which he came to the throne of Egypt, 53. Mr. Basil H. Cooper on circumstances in his reign, 54. Time of his reign, 60
Othniel, extinguishes the rule of Chusan-Risathaim the Cushite, 22
Oxus, called also the Gihon, 47

PALESTINE, rule of the nations of, over the Israelites, a necessity for the Egyptians, 58
Pamer, traditional sojourn of the Aryan, or Japhetic race in the highland

PET

of, near the sources of the Oxus and Indus, in Thibet, 10
Panodorus, the probable author of 'Sothis,' or 'The Dogstar,' 103 *note*. His mode of treating his work, 103. Anything but an ignoramus, 103 *note*
Passover, eclipse of the moon in B.C., 1, 4
Patriarchs, lists of, before and after the Flood, 2. Sum total of the duration of lives assigned to the, together with the one recorded son in each case, 3. Each patriarch possibly represents a successive historical period, 22
Paul, St., his explanations respecting the period of Hebrew servitude, 12. Meets with Gaius, Aquila, and Priscilla at Corinth, 82. His correction of a date in the first Book of Kings, 27. His statement in detail, 27, 28. Spends three years in Arabia, 80. With St. Peter founds the Church at Antioch, 82. His journey with Barnabas to Judæa, 82. Date of his conversion, 82. With St. Peter at Jerusalem, with St. James for fifteen days, 82. His stay of two years at Ephesus, 82. His last journey to Jerusalem, 82. His departure from Cæsarea, arrival in Rome, and martyrdom, 82. His dates, and the sources of his information, 86. Draws from an unwritten tradition, 82
Pekah of Israel attacks Ahaz of Judah, 41. Who is succoured by Tiglat Pilesar, King of Assyria, 41. Years of his reign, 41. Contemporary with Tiglat Pilesar, 41
Peleg, date of, 2
Persian monarchy, Darius Hystaspes-Vashtaspa the real founder of the monarchy, 62. Extent of his possessions, 62. Division of the empire into Satrapies, 62
Peter, St., regarded as one of the seven 'pillars' as well as 'the rock,' 3 *note*. Thrown into prison, from which he escapes marvellously, 79. Leaves Jerusalem for Rome, 79. His journey to Rome, 80. At the house of Mary, the mother of John Mark, where he is announced by Rhoda, 80. Flees for his life, and goes probably by Joppa and Cæsarea to Rome, 80. Founds the Church at Rome, 80, 81. First meets Simon Magus at Cæsarea, and 'drives him away unto Italy,' 80. Follows Simon, and has disputations with him at Rome, 80, 81. Meets with Philo of Alexandria in Rome, 81. St. Peter's familiar

PET

conversation with him, 81. St. Peter proclaims the Gospel in Rome, 81. Year of his arrival in Rome, 81. With St. Paul founds the Church at Antioch, 82. His martyrdom, perhaps contemporaneous with that of St. Paul, 82. With St. Paul and St. James at Jerusalem for fifteen days, 82. Instructed to proclaim the more perfect divine knowledge which had been whispered into their ears, 82

Petubastes, King of Egypt, reign of, 50, 60. Length of time from him to Shishak, 60. Assumed date of his accession to the throne, 52–54, 60. Reign of his dynasty, 59

Pharaoh of Joseph, one of the Hyksos kings, 13. The title given by him to Joseph, 14

Pharaoh of the exodus, Amenophis I., name of, according to Manetho, 15. Date of his death according to Orosius and to Manetho, 25, 26, 56, 84

Pharaoh of Hebrew bondage, Egyptian name of, according to Manetho, 15. The name Bokhoris given to the last Pharaoh by Orosius, 25 note

Pharaohs, list of the, contemporary with the foreign rulers in Israel, 57. The title of Pharaoh as understood in Egypt, 61

Pharisees, their belief respecting the Temple of Jerusalem, 75. Appear with the high priests before Pilato about the resurrection of Jesus, 76

Philistines, the, attack Ahaz of Judah, who is succoured by Tiglat Pilesar, 41. Their rule in Israel a necessity for the Egyptians, 57, 58. The Pharaohs and the, 57. Synchronisms of their rule with Egyptian campaigns, 57. Synchronism of the Philistine rule in Israel and the last twenty years of Ramesses III. 58. And of the fourth last period of the Philistine rule over the Israelites with the first year of Sothos I., 58. The Philistine dominion over the Israelites contemporaneous with the advances of the Pharaohs through Canaan into Mesopotamia, 60

Philo of Alexandria at Rome, where he has familiar conversation with St. Peter, 81. Questioned in the fourth century, 81. Date of his visit to Rome, 81. At the head of a deputation of Alexandrian Jews, which appear before Caligula, 81. His apology read before the Roman Senate in the

PUL

reign of Claudius, 81. Calls Thamar 'the stranger' in Israel, 110

Phtha, the Egyptian Hephaistos, 102

Pillars, the bridge with seven, 3

Pleiades, the author's shortly appearing work on 'the Pleiades and the Zodiac in their relations to biblical symbolism,' 8 note, 17 note, 89 note. Discovery of the connection of the, with the calendar, 8 note

— periods, 8, 89

Polyhistor, Alexander, confirms a tradition respecting Pul, King of Assyria, 40. Access to the writings of Berosus, 40

Pontius Pilate arrives in Rome after the death of Tiberius, 77 note. Sent there by Vitellius, who was governor of Syria, 77 note

Poole, R. S., Mr., reference to, 7

Prætorian rule, first year of, 81

Priscilla meets with St. Paul at Corinth, 82. Leaves Rome about 49–50, 82

Prophet Samuel the introducer of the prophet-schools in Israel, 55. The prophetic order acknowledges him, 55. See Corr. and Add. 'Children of them which killed the prophets,' 115

Psammetikh, reign of, 60

Psammus, reign of, 60

Pausennes II., King of Egypt, 53. His treaty with Shishak I., 54. Co-regent with Shishak I., Mr. Cooper's remarks on, 106. Years assigned by Manetho to him, 107. Reign of, 108

Ptolemæus, Claudius, his list of Assyrian kings, 32. The fragments of the Ptolemæan Canon known to us, 36, 87

Pul, King of Assyria, receives tribute from Menahem, King of Israel, 33. His name not found in Assyrian annals, 33. Called by God to punish Israel, 34. Date of his reign, 34. His expedition to Syria, 34. Date of his accession to the throne, 35. The first king of a new Assyrian dynasty, 36. Length of time of the second Assyrian dynasty, 37. The first year of Nabopalassar, 37. Possibility of the name being derived from Taklat-Habal-Asar, 39. Deposed as the last king of the first Assyrian dynasty, or raised by force as a king unconnected with the first dynasty, 39, 40. Tradition respecting him transmitted by Alexander Polyhistor, 40. Contemporaries, 44. Not Vullush, 44. See Corr. and Add.

PUR

Purim, events which led to the first feast of, 65. Date of the first feast, 117
Purusata, or Pulusata, their rule over Israel, 57

QUANDT, his essay 'Chronologisch-geographische Beiträge,' referred to, 66 *note*. On the death of Herod, 69, 70 *note*
Quirinus (Cyrenius), Roman governor of Syria, 67. Was not governor, but Varus, was in Syria, 68. Birth of Jesus when Quirinus was governor, 69, 70

RAMESSES I., date of his accession to the throne, 55
— II., inscription to, in Tanis-Avaris, 13. Date of his accession, 56. Years of his reign, 57. His reign synchronizes with the rule of the Midianites over the Israelites, 58
— III., date of his accession to the throne, attacks Maka-Tyra, 57. Road by which he went, 57. Years of his reign, and of his immediate successors, 57. The twenty years following the death of, synchronize with the Philistine rule in Israel, 57. Makes alliances with the Philistines and the Sharutana, 58
Ra's father, Phtha, the Egyptian Hephaistos, 102
Ramoth-Gilead, battle of, 33, 98, 99
Rampses (Ramesses?). *See* Ramesses I., II., and III.
Raphia, battle of, 59
Rathos, reign of, 106
Rawlinson, Sir Henry, 62 *note*
Rawlinson's Herodotus, 52 *note*, &c.
Recapitulation of the main points of our investigation, 30, 83, 91
'Rechab,' the Keys of St. Peter, or the history of, 109 *note*. Priesthood promised to the sons of, 111
Rechabites, the Jehovistic 'strangers,' their ethnical connections with David, Jethro, and Melchizedek, 25. Rechabites, 'strangers in Israel,' 110. But worshippers in the Temple, 110. Followed the Hebrews into exile, 111. Pointed out by Jeremiah as patterns to Israel, 111. Promised an eternal priesthood, 114
Rehoboam, his intended coronation at Shechem, 33. Jerusalem captured in the reign of, 42
Renouf, Mr. Lapage, 101 *note*

SAR

Reubenites, led into captivity by Tiglat Pilesar, 33
Reu, date of, 2
Rezin of Damascus attacks Ahaz of Judah, 41. Ahaz succoured by Tiglat Pilesar, King of Assyria, 41. Driven by the Assyrians to a city where he may have met with his death, 41
Rhoda announces St. Peter at the house of Mary the mother of John Mark, 80
Riblah, the high priest Serajah slain at, 112
Rock, St. Peter regarded as the, 3 *note*. A symbolical expression for the Holy Ghost, 3 *note*
Roman empire, censuses ordered by the Emperor Augustus to be taken of the, 66, 67. Rome, foundation of the church at, 80-82. Philo in, 81
Rougé, Vicomte de, not convinced of the truth of a new reading, 100 *note*, 102 *note*. On the Banner name of Shishak I., 106

SABAKO, or Sevek, slain by Tirhakah of Ethiopia, 51. Co-regent with Zeth-Sethos, 51
Sadducees, their belief respecting the Temple of Jerusalem, 76. Follow Jesus in his allegorical form of speech, 76
Saïtes, the first of the Hyksos Kings, 13. The twenty-sixth or second Saite Dynasty, 60
Salah, date of, 2
Salmanassur, date of the reign of, 32
Samaria, the city of, taken and destroyed by Sargon, and the date of the event, 42
Samaritan chronology, first date of the most ancient Samaritan tradition for the creation of the world, 10. This date a purely astronomical one, 10
Samaritan Flood, the year of the, 10
Samaritans assist in finishing the Temple, which is consecrated, 63
Samuel, first Book of, St. Paul and Josephus on the chronology of the, 28. Length of his office as judge, 28. Contemporary of the Royal High-Priest Smendes in Egypt, 55. The introducer of prophet schools in Israel, 55. Years from the division of the land until the time of, 85, 86.
Saosduchinus, date of his reign, 32
Sargon, his statement as to 350 of his ancestors reigning over the Assyrians, 9, 10 *note*, 48. His assertion probably correct, 9. Date of his reign, 32. Imposes tribute on the Hebrews

SAU

not at Lakish but at Jerusalem, 35.
'The destroyer of the city of Samaria and the entire Beth-Omri,' 42. Makes Hosea a prisoner, 42. Hezekiah rules contemporaneously with Sargon, 42. Makes an expedition to Ashdod, 42. His son and successor Sennacherib leads the vanguard of the Assyrians, and enters the territory of Judah before Sargon, 42. His campaign to Judah, 43. Rules for at least three years as the Arkaiunos of the Ptolemæan Canon at Babylon, 43. Deposes Mardok Empados, the Merodach Baladan of the Babylonian annals, 43. Besieges and imposes a tribute on Jerusalem, which Sennacherib enforces ten years later, 43. Rules for three years in Babylon, 43. Contemporary with Hezekiah of Judah, 44. Subdues Ashdod and Judah, 59. Distinguishes Sevek as Sultani from the Pharaoh, 59. Transports the chief Daiuccu to Hamath, 109
Saul, forty years assigned to, in the Acts, 28. Years of his reign, 86
Saul-mugina, date of the reign of, 32
Sayce, Mr., on Jehu, 20. On Sargon before Jerusalem, 35, 43. On Merodach-Nimrod, 47. On Deiokes and Daiuccu, 108, 109
Sebennytus, city of, Manetho a priest of, 50
Sennacherib, the Assyrians under, according to Herodotus, 21. Date of the reign of, 32. Refers in Isaiah as to cities overthrown by Assyria, 34. Takes to Nineveh Hezekiah's 'precious molten metal,' 35. His period of 600 years before his capture of Babylon, 36. Leads the vanguard of his father's army and enters Judah before Sargon, 42. Contemporary with Hezekiah, 44. The myth of the mice gnawing the bow-strings and shield-thongs of the Assyrians, and the miracle of the destruction of the Assyrian army in a night, 51. Comes into conflict with Ipsabara (? 'Αστι-βάρας), 109
Sephôris, Judas of, his revolt of the people at, 68. The city wasted by Varus, 68
Septuagint, instruction of Jesus in the, during his stay in Egypt, 78
Seraja, identified with Sirach or Soirach, 112. Slain at Riblah, 112. The name, 112
Serpent, symbol of the, among the Medes and Hyksos, 19

SHA

Serubbabel not mentioned by Ezra, 63. Foundations of the Temple and of the walls laid under, 63. His acts condemned by Ezekiel, but approved by Jeremiah, 112. Pointed out as God's chosen instrument, 115
Serug, date of, 2
Setaapethi-Nubti, name of in an inscription to, in Tanis-Avaris, which he rebuilt, 13
Seth, date of, 2. Contemporary with Adam, 4. Age of his father when he was begotten, 4. The national god of the Hyksos, 13. Temple to, at Tanis, 13. The serpent the symbol of, and the origin of the name of the Hyksos, 14. Possible historical period represented by, 92
Sethos I., son of the Amenophis of the exodus, 15. Length of his reign according to the monuments, 55
— The first year of, synchronizes with the fourth last period of the Philistine rule over the Israelites, 58. Sethos overruns Syria, 58. See also Zeth
Seti I., his name of Arnimos, 101 note. Reigns with his father Menophres Ramses I., 101 note
Sevek gives up Yavani of Ashdod to Sargon, 59
— I. burns Bokhoris II. alive, 60. See Sabaco
'Seven chiefs of the Persians and Medes,' possible connection of the seven conspirators and the, 62 note
Seven, early and aboriginal connection of the number, with the seven stars of the Pleiades, 71 note, 90
Seventy years of Jeremiah, type of the, 7. Mystic number of, for the seven days of the creation of the universe, 7
Shah, Khsha, derivation of the word, 62
Shalmaneser II., King of Assyria, his campaign against Benhadad of Damascus and his confederates, 33. And against Haznel and Jehu, 33. Contemporary with Ahab of Israel, 44
— IV., Hosea contemporary with for five years, 42, 44
Sharpe, Mr., his 'Chronology of the Bible' referred to, 97. His important discovery in Hebrew chronology, 97, 98
Sharutana, allies of the enemies of Ramesses II. and III., 57. Assist the Tsakruri and other enemies against the Egyptians, 57. Their rule over Israel, 57. Make an alliance with the Egyptians, 58

SHE

Shem, date of, 2. Receives a tradition from Methuselah and transmits it to Jacob, 3. Historical importance of the date of the birth of, implied in Genesis to have taken place in b.c. 2,458, 11. Starting-point of Hebrew Chronology, 11. Necessary ethnic interpretation of what in Genesis is called the birth of, 17. First settlements of the Shemites in Mesopotamia, 16. Professor J. G. Müller on the Shemites in their relations to Hamites and Japhetites, 17 note
Sheshonk I., his conquest of Judah, 50. Years of his divided reign, 60. His sole reign, 60
Shiddim, Abraham's defeat of Chedorlaomer in the vale of, 12. Date of the battle of, 12, 13, 19, 84
Shinar, first historical inhabitants of, 16. Probably so called by the Assyrians, 18. Peopled by Japhetites and Hamites, 18. The 'sumir' of cuneiform inscriptions, 18. The first historical inhabitants of Shinar-Babylonia, 21. The Japhetites settle in Shinar-Babylonia, 23. The Hebrews regarded as Indians from the East to Shinar, where Iranian Medes joined them, 24. From the land of Shinar Ashur 'went forth and built Nineveh,' 24
Shishak I., contemporary in harmony with the Bible account, 29. Contemporary with Solomon and Jeroboam, 50. Number of years according to Manetho from Shishak to Petubastes, 50. Duration of the Shishak dynasty, and date of the end of his reign, 53. Became king of entire Egypt, 54. His accession to the throne at Bubastis, 54. Flight of Jeroboam to the court of Shishak, 55. His capture of Jerusalem, 55. In possession of undisputed power in Egypt, 55. Year when he came to the throne, 58. The regnal years from Shishak to Amos, and from Shishak to Amasis, 58. The established synchronism between Solomon and Shishak, 87. Complementary double tradition to the length of the reign of, 107. His banner name, 107. Co-regent with Psusennes II., Mr. Cooper's remarks on, 106. Years of his reign, 108
Sidon, Japhetites and Hamites at, whence they went towards Shinar, 18
Silsilis inscription, the, 50. The in-

SYN

scription referred to respecting Shishak I., 108.
Simon (Magus ?), rising under, 77 note
Simon Magus, Peter meets him at Cæsarea, and drives 'him away unto Italy,' 80. Their disputations in Rome, 81
Simplicius, the philosopher, transmits the statement of Callisthenes as to the astronomical calculations of the Chaldæans, 46. Flees to Chosroës, King of the Persians, 46
Sir-inadin-pal, date of the reign of, 32
Sirach, or Seirach, identified with the high priest Seraja, 113
Sirius, the rising of, the *dies solennis* of the Egyptians, 100. Date of the rising, 100, 101.
Smendes, first of the royal high priests of Tanis, came to the throne, 55
Smith, G., Mr., his date of the first Assyrian capture of Babylon, 36. His 'chronology of Sennacherib' referred to, 14
Smith, Dr., Dictionary of the Bible, vii
Smyth, Piazzi, his 'Life and Work at the Great Pyramid' referred to, 8 note
Solomon, contemporary in harmony with the Bible account, 29. Date of the death of, 29, 33. Years of the reign of, 86. The established synchronism between Solomon and Shishak, 87. Date for his accession, 97, 98
'Sothis-Book,' in the Syncelline Canon, 101
'Sothis,' or 'The Dogstar,' a forged work of Manetho, 103. The Pseudo-Manethonian, a variant in, 107
Stephen, St., year of the martyrdom of, 79
Stranger in Israel, 24, *app. note* vii
Suetonius mentions the bronze tablets with public acts of Augustus at Rome, 67
Sun, Ammu the Assyrian name of the, 20
Sun-dial, retrogression of the, the wonder which was done in the land, 43. The sun-dial of Ahaz introduced to the Hebrews as an Assyrian innovation, 43. A Babylonian one replaces the Assyrian one above, mentioned, 44
Syncellus, Vice-Patriarch of Constantinople about 800, on the date of Solomon's temple, the fall of Troy, and the foundation of Carthage, 29 note. Records thirty-four years for the reign of Shishak I., 53
Synchronisms from the Hebrew and Egyptian chronology, 86

INDEX.

TAB

TABLES, chronological, from the birth of Shem to the destruction of Solomon's temple, *folding sheet*
Tabarnka, reign of, 60
Tanis-Avaris, or Zoan, inscription to Ramesses II. in, 13. Rebuilt by Setaapethi-Nubti, 13. Date of the rebuilding of, 13, 14. The foreign rulers, or Hyksos, driven out of by Ahmes, assisted by Admiral Ahmes, 16. Re-occupied by the Israelites after the Hyksos were expelled, 25. Double attack on, one under Ahmes and one under Amenophis I., 26. Final expulsion of the Hyksos from Avaris and Egypt, 26. The first of the royal high priests of, Smendes, came to the throne, 55
Targumist, reverence in which he was held, 113
Taxing first made when Cyrenius (Quirinus) was governor of Syria, 67
Teacher, required age of a, or master, 74
Tefnacht (including Piankhi), reign of, 60
Temple, date of Nebuchadnezzar's destruction of the, 4. Finish and consecration of the newly-built Temple, 4. Historical events which led to it, 5. Table of the first half of the 7,000 years, or from the destruction of the first Temple to the creation of heaven and earth, 7. Period from the exodus to the foundation of the Temple, 8. Incorrectness of the Biblical date between the exodus and the foundation of the Temple, 27. The mistake corrected by St. Paul and Josephus, 27, 28. Date of Solomon's Temple, 29. Date of the consecration of the second Temple, 61. Date of the foundation of the Temple and of the walls, 62. With the help of the Samaritans the Temple is finished and consecrated, 63
Terah, date of, 2, 14
Testament, New, not finally revised before the time of Constantine, 71
Testament, Old, designed alterations detected in the Hebrew text of the, 71
Thamar, called by Philo 'the stranger,' and married to Judah, 110
Thebes, temple of, stone cut in Upper Egypt for the, 50
Theocracy, date of the restoration of the, 5
Thibet, traditional sojourn of the Aryan or Japhetic race on the highland of Pamer in, 10

TSA

Thothmes the Great, on the date of the accession of, by Mr. Basil H. Cooper, 100
— III., reign of, 104. His regnal years, 104 *note*. The day of his death, 104 *note*
Tinaken, King of Thebes, 14
Tiberius, reign of, 74. Death of, according to 'annals' of Tacitus, 74. The crucifixion takes place in the reign of, 77. Length of his reign, 77. His death before Pontius Pilate had arrived in Rome, 77 *note*. Year of his death, 77
Tiglat Pilesar, date of reign of, 32. Receives tribute from King Menahem of Israel, 33. Leads into captivity the Reubenites, Gadites, and the half tribe of Manasseh, 33. Date of his reign, 34. Makes no mention of his parentage, contrary to custom, 39. Conclusion therefore that he was not of royal descent, 39. Synchronism between him and Azariah, or Uzziah of Judah, 40. Annexes several districts of Hamath with their cities, which in 'faithless rebellion' had gone over to 'Azariah (Uzziah) of Judah.' 41. Receives tribute from Ahaz of Judah, whom he succours against several enemies, 41
— — IV., contemporary with Ahaz of Judah and Pekah of Israel, 44
Tirhakah, King of Ethiopia, his advance against the Hebrews, accompanied by pestilence, 44. His advance into Egypt with a vast army, 51. Slays Sevek or Sabako, 51, 52. Contemporary with Sethos and four Assyrian kings, 51. He sues for peace, 52. Date when he slew Sevek, 53, 59
Tradition, 'holy,' the bridge of seven pillars, 3. Of the patriarchs, 3. Begun to be recorded in the time of Moses, 3
Tradition, hereditary tribal, first verbal and then written, 9, 88. Eastern origin of this tradition, 88. Occasionally symbols or rules of faith were formed by stewards of tradition, 88. Existence of, in pre-historic times, 9. A verbal tradition the highest privilege of the highest class, 9
Troy, date of the fall of, 29 *note*
Troas, mice revered by the people of, 52 *note*. Reason for this, 52 *note*
Tsafento, 'sustainer or feeder of the world,' King Kames of Thebes mentioned on the monuments as, 14
Tsakruri, the, join the Sharutana against the Egyptians, 57

INDEX.

TUK

Tuklat-Habal-Asar, the name Pul might be derived from, 39, 40
Tuthmoses (Thot-Moses), the name of the Pharaoh of Hebrew bondage, 15
— of Manetho, assumed to refer to Ahmes, 25
— I., his reign, 84
— II., Pharaoh of Egypt, years of his reign, 57, 84
— III., reign of, 26. Accession of, 56, 84, 100. Years of his reign, 57
Tyre. *See* Maka-Tyra

UR of the Chaldees, the dwelling-place of the ancestors of Abraham, 16
Urukh rules over the Assyrians, 18. Date of the reign of, 20. His expulsion of the Berosian Medes from Babylon, 19. The post-Median dynasty of, 21. The date of Urukh fixed by a cuneiform inscription, 37. Urukh the builder of the Tower of Babel, 37. A period of 700 years from Urukh to Hammurabi, 37. His house of Bel at Babel, 37. The cylinder of Nabonadius, 37. Confirmation of period of 1903 years from Urukh to Darius Codomannus, 46. Date of his accession, 46. His tower of 'the seven lights of the earth' at Borsippa, 47

VARRO, on the date of the Noachian flood, 11
Varus, Roman governor of Syria, 68. Wastes the city of Sephôris, 68
Vashtaspa, the name of, 62
Vashti, the name of, 62. Meaning of the name of, 62 *note*
Victorinus or Victorius of Aquitania, first fixes the Christian era in 465, 72
Vistáspa, meaning of, 62 *note*
— Chavanian, in Bactra, 9 *note*
Volkmar, his investigation respecting John the Baptist, 72 *note*

ZOR

WILKINSON, Sir Gardner, reference to, 52 *note*.

XERXES, meaning of the name, 61. His queen-mother Atossa in the 'Persians' of Aeschylus is Hadassah or Esther, 62
Xoite Dynasty in Lower Egypt, 103

YAVANI of Ashdod, besieged by Sargon, King of Assyria, 59. Given up to Sargon, 59
Year, the Egyptian primitive, 100 *note*

ZADOK, of the line of Eleazar, 111. The Divine command that the sons of Zadok only should stand before God, 111
Zechariah, the prophet, speaks of a future fall of Babylon, described in the Apocalypse, 6. The seven visions of, 63. Explanation of the visions, 63. One of the visions of, referring to Joshua and his antagonist, 110. A stranger in Israel, 116. His father Berechaiah, 116
Zend-Avesta, or tradition written, 18. People of the, 23. No trace of Semitic words in the, 23
Zerubbabel, historical events which led to the building of the second Temple under, 5. Knowledge of the initiated contemporaries of, of the millennium, 6
Zeth, King of Egypt, the Sethos of Herodotus, 51. Contemporary reigns, with Chr. Tables. Possesses a fleet in the Mediterranean, 53. His death, 53, 59, 60. Years of his reign, 59, 60. *See* Seth
Zoan. *See* Tanis-Avaris.
Zoroaster, in whose time 'men began to publish the name of Jehovah,' 9 *note*.
Zoroaster, first King at Babylon of the Medes from the Caspian, 23. So called from the great monotheist, 23, 49

By the same Author.

THE
HIDDEN WISDOM OF CHRIST
AND THE KEY OF KNOWLEDGE,
OR
HISTORY OF THE APOCRYPHA.

2 vols. 8vo. (1865) price 28*s*.

'The problem of the formation of Christian doctrines may be regarded as solved.'
REVUE DES DEUX MONDES.

THE KEYS OF SAINT PETER,
OR
THE HOUSE OF RECHAB CONNECTED WITH THE HISTORY OF SYMBOLISM AND IDOLATRY.

8vo. (1867) price 14*s*.

GOD IN HISTORY;
OR
THE PROGRESS OF MAN'S FAITH IN THE MORAL ORDER OF THE WORLD.

BY THE LATE BARON BUNSEN, D.PH. D.C.L. D.D.

TRANSLATED FROM THE GERMAN BY SUSANNAH WINKWORTH;
WITH A
PREFACE BY A. P. STANLEY, D.D. DEAN OF WESTMINSTER.

3 vols. 8vo. price 42*s*.

PRAYERS
FROM
THE COLLECTION OF THE LATE BARON BUNSEN.

SELECTED AND TRANSLATED BY CATHERINE WINKWORTH.

Fcp. 8vo. price 3*s*. 6*d*.

London: LONGMANS & CO.

www.ingramcontent.com/pod-product-compliance
Lightning Source LLC
Chambersburg PA
CBHW030334170426
43202CB00010B/1121